AF882358

Pakistan's Cotton and Textile Economy

Intersectoral Linkages and Effects on Rural and Urban Poverty

Caesar B. Cororaton and David Orden

RESEARCH REPORT 158

INTERNATIONAL FOOD POLICY RESEARCH INSTITUTE
sustainable solutions for ending hunger and poverty
IFPRI®

International Food Policy Research Institute
2033 K Street, NW
Washington, D.C. 20006-1002, U.S.A.
Telephone +1-202-862-5600
www.ifpri.org

DOI: 10.2499/9780896291676RR158

Library of Congress Cataloging-in-Publication Data

Cororaton, Caesar B. (Caesar Bucia), 1958–
Pakistan's cotton and textile economy : intersectoral linkages and effects on rural and urban poverty / Caesar B. Cororaton and David Orden. — Rev.
p. cm. — (IFPRI research report ; 158)
Includes bibliographical references.
ISBN 978-0-89629-167-6 (alk. paper)
1. Textile industry—Pakistan. 2. Cotton trade—Pakistan. 3. Poverty—Pakistan. 4. Pakistan—Economic conditions. I. Orden, David. II. International Food Policy Research Institute. III. Title. IV. Series: Research report (International Food Policy Research Institute) ; 158.
HD9866.P32C67 2008
338.4'76770095491—dc22 2008036765

Contents

Tables

Figures

Boxes

Foreword

The economy of Pakistan is highly dependent on its cotton and textile sectors, which face significant challenges and opportunities in an environment of fluctuating world prices, macroeconomic instability, and changes in the global trade regime for textiles and apparel. Yet there is limited systematic analysis available that can help us understand the linkages between these sectors and the effects of their performance on the country's economy.

Using an economywide computable general equilibrium model integrated with a national household survey, this study conducts simulations of several recent and prospective factors affecting the cotton and textile sectors and analyzes their impacts on rural and urban poverty. One set of policy simulations addresses the effects arising from shocks that are largely external—changes in foreign savings that affect the exchange rate and therefore the competitiveness of Pakistan's exports of textiles and other products, and changes in world prices that shift its terms of trade. A second set of simulations analyzes the effects resulting largely from domestic policies and investments, such as government subsidies to the textile industry and productivity improvements in the cotton and textile sectors. The study traces the effects in each scenario through transmission channels from output and factor supplies and demands, through commodity and factor prices, to household incomes, welfare, and levels of poverty.

The analysis of a large inflow of foreign savings, as occurred during 2001–06, sheds light on the importance of the country's macroeconomic circumstances, which are also relevant given the financial instability currently facing Pakistan. The terms-of-trade analysis demonstrates a poverty-reducing effect of higher cotton prices that is relevant to understanding the income-distribution effects in Pakistan of the wide fluctuations in world commodity markets. The analysis of higher productivity shows positive long-term dynamic gains that can help guide policymakers in reallocating resources—from support of the textile industry through various direct subsidies to capacity-building public investments that are badly needed to improve Pakistan's international competitiveness.

I hope that the insights drawn from this study will be useful inputs into policy discussions in Pakistan and elsewhere.

Joachim von Braun
Director General, IFPRI

Acknowledgments

This report is one of three main outputs from a research project titled "Pakistan-India: Cotton Trade Policy and Poverty Study" undertaken by the International Food Policy Research Institute (IFPRI) and its collaborators from October 2005 to June 2007. The other two reports are *Cotton-Textile-Apparel Sectors of Pakistan: Situation and Challenges Faced* (2008) by Caesar B. Cororaton, Abdul Salam, Zafar Altaf, and David Orden and *Cotton-Textile-Apparel Sectors of India: Situation and Challenges Faced* (2008) by Jatinder S. Bedi and Caesar B. Cororaton. The research project was supported by the Agriculture and Rural Development Sector Unit, South Asia Region, of the World Bank.

We thank Paul Dorosh, the project manager for the World Bank, for his advice and encouragement throughout the study. We also thank Dr. Sohail Malik, president of Innovative Development Strategies, Ltd. (IDS), Islamabad, for his support and facilitation of the efforts of the investigators. We thank Dr. Munir Ahmad, Pakistan Agriculture Research Council, and Rizwana Siddiqui, Pakistan Institute for Development Economics (PIDE), for facilitating training workshops in computable general equilibrium models, which were held at PIDE in Islamabad in March and July 2006 as one activity of the project. We also gratefully acknowledge the financial support of the Netherlands Ministry of Foreign Affairs through the Bank-Netherlands Partnership Program trust fund of the World Bank. Finally we thank Shirley Raymundo and Joy Fabela, administrative coordinators at IFPRI, for their assistance in the preparation of the report.

The results included in this report have previously been presented at two professional meetings (American Agricultural Economics Association, July 2006, and Pakistan Society of Development Economists, December 2006); at several policy outreach/discussion meetings with industry, academic, and government representatives in Pakistan (Islamabad Club, Islamabad, December 2006; Punjab Ministry of Commerce, Lahore, December 2006); at seminars at IFPRI (Washington, D.C., U.S.A., January and April 2007; New Delhi, India, April 2007), the World Bank (September 2007), and the University of Guelph (June 2008); at the Conference on Rural Development and Poverty, hosted by PIDE in Islamabad, Pakistan (April 2007); at the World Bank Workshop on Effects of Agricultural Price Distortions on Growth, Income Distribution, and Poverty, in West Lafayette, Indiana, U.S.A. (June 2007); and at a conference of the Poverty Reduction, Equity, and Growth Network, in Berlin, Germany (September 2007). We thank Antoine Bouët, Betina Dimaranan, and Marcelle Thomas at IFPRI and participants at the seminars and conferences for helpful suggestions and comments. We hope workshops can be organized in 2009 for representatives of industry, government, and academe in Islamabad, in collaboration with IDS, and in New Delhi, in collaboration with the National Council of Applied Economic Research.

Acronyms and Abbreviations

ATC	Agreement on Textiles and Clothing
CEC	Cotton Export Corporation
CES	constant elasticity of substitution
CET	constant elasticity of transformation
CGE	computable general equilibrium
FAO	Food and Agriculture Organization of the United Nations
FGT	Foster-Greer-Thorbecke
HIES	Household Integrated Economic Survey
ICAC	International Cotton Advisory Committee
IDS	Innovative Development Strategies, Ltd.
IFPRI	International Food Policy Research Institute
MEP	minimum export price
MFA	Multi-Fiber Agreement
SAM	social accounting matrix
SITC	Standard International Trade Classification
TFP	total factor productivity
USDA	U.S. Department of Agriculture
WTO	World Trade Organization

Summary

The cotton, textile, and apparel industries—which are critical sectors of the Pakistan economy and important determinants of rural and urban poverty—face challenges that include instability in the world prices of cotton, liberalization of multilateral trade of textiles and clothing since 2004, and strengthening of the currency arising from a surge in foreign capital inflows and remittances since 2001. Using a computable general equilibrium (CGE) model calibrated to a 2001–02 social accounting matrix of the Pakistan economy and linked to the 2001–02 Pakistan Household Integrated Economic Survey, this report conducts simulation experiments and analyzes the intersectoral and poverty implications of (1) an increase in foreign savings inflows into Pakistan; (2) an increase in world prices of cotton lint and yarn, textiles, or a combination of these; (3) a government production subsidy to one of the cotton-related sectors; and (4) an improvement in total factor productivity (TFP) in one or more of these sectors.

Simulation 1 analyzes the effects on competitiveness, particularly for the cotton and textile industries, through an appreciation of the real exchange rate that results from the surge in foreign capital inflows. The results indicate that increased capital inflows raise real investment and household income and reduce poverty in Pakistan, but the tradable sectors (particularly the cotton and textile sectors) contract, and the incomes of farmers decline. Under conditions of capital outflow, as started to occur in 2008 owing to political turmoil in Pakistan and rising world food and oil prices, our simulations would imply effects the reverse of those modeled herein.

Simulation 2 analyzes the effects of an increase in world cotton and textile prices. Historical indicators show wide cotton lint price fluctuations; cotton fabric prices move to reflect the raw material price as well as for other reasons. Production and exports in Pakistan improve under positive sectoral price shocks, with greater benefits to farmers (particularly cotton households) and rural areas from an increase in cotton prices. There are indirect adverse intersectoral effects between the cotton and textile sectors, as a boom in either sector causes the exchange rate to appreciate.

The textile industry is backed by a strong and powerful association that lobbies for government support and subsidies. Simulation 3 analyzes the effects of a government subsidy to the industry. The financing of the subsidy in the analysis is either through a compensatory consumption tax or through a compensatory income tax. The subsidy leads to an overall decrease in welfare in both cases. It will increase poverty if the financing is through an additional consumption tax because of the upward taxation effect on consumer prices. However, it will reduce poverty if the financing is through an income tax, in which case the burden of additional taxation falls only on urban non-poor households, creating an indirect transfer from the urban non-poor to other household groups.

Liberalization of the world trade in textiles and clothing resulting from ending the quota-based Multi-Fiber Agreement in 2004 has affected world prices and trade patterns of cotton lint and yarn, textiles, and apparel. This will test Pakistan's ability to compete in world markets. Pakistan can best take advantage of this shift if it improves its competitiveness through higher productivity. Simulation 4 examines cases of higher industry TFP in raw cotton, cotton lint and yarn, and textiles in both the short and long run using a dynamic-recursive version of the CGE model. The increase in TFP is welfare-increasing, with dynamic effects and the level of impact among the cotton-textile sectors and across household groups depending on whether productivity improves in one or more of these highly interdependent sectors.

Overall the results of simulations 1 and 2 demonstrate different effects arising from two largely external positive shocks: the increase in foreign savings strengthens the currency and creates a boom in the nontrade sectors, whereas an increase in world cotton or textile prices improves Pakistan's terms of trade and generates a boom in these sectors in particular. An inflow of foreign savings depresses traded sectors but stimulates investment and expanded production of nontraded goods. Because of the large share of the cotton-related sectors in overall exports, an export boom in these sectors also strengthens the currency, which negatively affects other tradables and the domestic currency value of household income from any given level of foreign remittances.

These different effects must be understood by policymakers trying to assess, for example, the performance of the cotton, yarn, and textile sectors and their impacts on employment and poverty. These impacts must be evaluated in light of more liberalized trade rules, the capital inflow or increase in foreign remittances that occurred during 2000–06, the decline in world cotton prices in the 1990s, and the reversal of these circumstances that has recently been evident. Simulations 3 and 4 are relevant to policymakers who must direct limited domestic resources to capacity-building public investments but who also face calls for more direct support from industry lobbies.

CHAPTER 1

Introduction

The cotton, textile, and apparel industries—which constitute the production of raw cotton, ginning, spinning, weaving, dyeing, printing, and garment manufacturing—contributed 11 percent of Pakistan's gross domestic product in 2004–05. They account for 46 percent of the entire manufacturing sector and employ 35 percent of the industrial labor force. Cotton is Pakistan's principal industrial crop, and it provides critical income to rural households. Cotton-based commodities, such as yarn, textiles, and clothing, provide 60 percent of the country's total export receipts.

These key sectors of the Pakistan economy face a number of challenges. In the international market, the price of cotton has been unstable around a generally declining long-term trend. In the yarn and textile sectors, multilateral trade rules have changed, and there is increased competition among exporters. Given the size of the industry and the high incidence of poverty in Pakistan, the implications of these developments for the poor are significant.

Using a computable general equilibrium (CGE) model calibrated to a 2001–02 social accounting matrix (SAM), this report examines how a number of developments in the international and domestic economies affect sectoral production, with a focus on the cotton-to-apparel value chain. We examine the effects on key macroeconomic indicators, sectoral output and factor demand, output and factor prices, and household income. Furthermore we examine the implications of these developments for poverty through a microsimulation linking the CGE model results to disaggregated data from the 2001–02 Pakistan Household Integrated Economic Survey (HIES) of the Federal Bureau of Statistics (2003).

The report is organized as follows. Chapters 2–4 provide the context for the analysis. Chapter 2 presents broad trends in the international cotton, textile, and apparel markets, highlighting the share of Pakistan in these markets over time. Chapter 3 presents key features of the cotton, textile, and apparel sectors in Pakistan and discusses major shifts in cotton and textile policies. Chapter 4 describes recent trends in rural and urban poverty in Pakistan. Together, these chapters provide a richly detailed context for the analysis that follows, offering insights for the model specification and complementing the model results, since the CGE model cannot capture all impacts on the diverse subsectors of cotton production, ginning, spinning, and weaving in as much detail.

The CGE model and the analysis of policy scenarios are presented in Chapters 5–9. Chapter 5 presents an overview of the model and its key parameters, with the model's full structure given in Appendix A. Chapter 6 describes the poverty assessment microsimulations. Chapter 7 gives the definition of four sets of policy-relevant simulations. The simulation results are presented in Chapters 8 and 9. A summary of the results and a discussion of conclusions are provided in Chapter 10.

Simulation 1 addresses the effects on competitiveness (particularly on the textile industry) through changes in the real exchange rate resulting from the surge in foreign capital inflows to Pakistan (more than 100 percent) from 2001 to 2007. Simulation 2 analyzes the effects of an increase in world prices of cotton lint and yarn, textiles, or a combination of these commodities, where historical indicators show wide fluctuations and cotton fabric prices tend to move with prices of cotton lint. Falling world cotton prices in the late 1990s raised concerns about lower farm incomes and increased rural poverty.

The textile industry in Pakistan is backed by a strong and powerful association that lobbies for government support and subsidies. Simulation 3 analyzes the effects of a government production subsidy to the industry on welfare and poverty using two alternative compensatory taxes: consumption versus income. Finally, a major shift in the international trading agreements on textiles and clothing has occurred with the lifting in 2005 of import quotas in restricted markets under the Multi-Fiber Agreement (MFA). The change in the trade regime will potentially affect world yarn, textile, and apparel prices and trade patterns, testing Pakistan's ability to compete in nonquota markets. Pakistan can best take advantage of this shift if it improves its competitiveness through higher productivity. Simulation 4 looks at the case of higher industry total factor productivity (TFP) sector by sector in the short and long run, using a dynamic-recursive version of the CGE model.

The results from the analysis are illustrative of the forces that will shape the cotton, textile, and apparel sectors in Pakistan in the coming years, and they demonstrate the effects of these forces on rural and urban poverty. The largest increase in household income and reduction of poverty arise from the modeled increase of foreign savings in simulation 1. The increase also results in significant improvement in overall investment. Appreciation of the exchange rate leads to a net reduction in exports and increase in imports, but there are offsetting favorable effects on the construction-related and service sectors. There is significant movement of resources, especially labor, toward these sectors and increases in the prices of factors they use heavily. Thus wages of skilled and unskilled labor improve, as do the average returns to capital. However, wages of farm labor and the average returns to land decline. All households, except rural farmers, benefit from incomes that are higher in the aggregate by 1.31 percent. Both urban and rural poverty decrease due to higher incomes and lower domestic prices.

The above analysis applies to a generally stable economic and political environment. However, the political turmoil arising in 2007 and 2008 from the firing of the Supreme Court judges, the assassination of the former prime minister, and the fall of the Musharraf administration may reverse the flow of foreign capital. This reversal, together with the widening foreign trade imbalance resulting from high world food and oil prices, may potentially lead to a crisis in the balance of payments that could unfavorably affect the real sector of the economy and therefore poverty. The results in simulation 1 involving a capital inflow are suggestive of the possible reverse effects that could occur in the context of a capital outflow.

Simulation 2 focuses on shocks with a sectoral origin. By itself, an increase in cotton lint and yarn or textile prices has several different effects. A 20 percent increase in the world prices of cotton lint and yarn—which is about the magnitude that would have offset the price decrease Pakistan industries experienced in the late 1990s—improves aggregate household income by 0.25 percent. Factors heavily used in raw cotton production, which are farm labor and land, command higher prices. Rural farmers benefit from higher income, while urban households as well as rural non-farmers experience lower income. There is a reduction in poverty for cotton-producing households in Punjab, Sindh, and other Pakistan.[1] There is an increase in poverty for non-cotton households in Sindh and other Pakistan, but a decrease in Punjab. The province of Punjab is the major producer of cotton. Thus the improvement in world cotton prices has favorable indirect effects on non-cotton households in Punjab.

The impact of higher cotton prices on textile production is negative, as the increase in the world price of cotton lint and yarn makes its export relatively attractive compared with domestic sales to the local industry. This finding highlights the dependence of the domestic textile industry on the availability of domestically produced raw materials. Alternatively a 5 percent increase in the world prices of textiles, which again would have offset the decrease in world prices in the late 1990s, increases total household income by 0.4 percent. There is an increase in output in the textile sector because of export growth. Because of the large share of textiles in the overall exports of the economy, this leads to a substantial appreciation of the exchange rate. The export sectors other than textiles become less competitive, including the cotton lint and yarn sector. Yarn imports increase, and lower output in the cotton lint and yarn sector translates into reduced demand for raw cotton. Rural farmers end up with lower income, while the rest of the household groups benefit from higher income. Overall poverty declines, with the decrease in urban poverty relatively more than the decrease in rural poverty.

Since world prices of cotton lint, yarn, and fabric have historically tended to move simultaneously, we also consider a joint scenario combining these price movements. The results are mutually reinforcing in terms of appreciation of the exchange rate. Raw cotton and cotton lint and yarn output and exports again increase, but production and exports of textiles and other traded goods fall. Real factor prices all increase but at various rates. The increase in the overall household income is 0.59 percent, which is higher than that under the previous two scenarios. The decline in overall poverty is also higher. There is also more of a decline in overall poverty.

Policymakers often face calls for subsidies from the textile industry. In simulation 3, although consumers benefit from a subsidy to the sector through the lower prices they pay and textile producers benefit through the higher prices they receive, the subsidy is welfare-reducing, whether financed through a compensatory consumption tax or a compensatory income tax. The increase in the consumer prices as a result of a higher consumption tax results in an increase in poverty. The use of an income tax will have significant effects in reducing poverty despite the reduction in overall welfare. This is because the burden of an income tax to finance the subsidy falls only on urban non-poor households. The rest of the household groups, especially the poor, benefit from the lower consumer price as a result of the subsidy and from an indirect income transfer from the urban non-poor.

The Pakistan cotton-textile-apparel industry is facing major challenges, especially in the world market. Prior to 2005 Pakistan enjoyed preferential treatment in cotton-textile trade under the MFA. However, with the abolition of the MFA in January 2005, the world demand for textiles became price responsive, making lower-cost producers more competitive. This presents an opportunity for Pakistan if it focuses on improving the competitiveness of the cotton-textile-apparel industry through enhanced productivity.

We address the implications for Pakistan of enhanced international competitiveness in the cotton-textile sectors by assess-

[1]Other Pakistan includes Azad Kashmir, Balochistan, the Northern Areas, the North-West Frontier Province, federally administered areas, and federally administered tribal areas.

ing the effects of exogenous improvements in TFP. Since improved TFP has long-term implications, we extend our CGE model into a dynamic-recursive form to capture the economywide effects over time. Specifically we generate a baseline scenario without TFP improvement from 2001 to 2027 assuming an increase in the labor supply of 2 percent per year. Sectoral capital stock is updated annually using a capital accumulation equation. The supply of land is fixed, but land use varies across agricultural sectors. In this analysis, we take 2008 as the first year in which a permanent improvement in productivity occurs. We evaluate three scenarios: (1) increasing by 5 percent the TFP for raw cotton production only; (2) increasing the TFP of the raw cotton and cotton lint and yarn sectors simultaneously, and (3) also increasing the TFP in textiles. For each scenario, we take the percent difference from the dynamic simulation results with and without TFP improvement and analyze the economywide and household income effects. Any increase in TFP is welfare-increasing. However, interesting insights can be drawn from the dynamic effects among the cotton-textile sectors and across household groups.

An improvement in TFP in the raw cotton sector alone increases production and drives down its domestic price. This is because raw cotton is not exported but is instead a raw material used in cotton lint and yarn production. The effects of the productivity improvement in raw cotton are therefore limited by the absorptive capacity of the cotton lint and yarn sector, which operates along its old production function because there is no corresponding increase in its TFP. Improved productivity in raw cotton immediately benefits the cotton lint and yarn sector and induces an inflow of capital. Output of cotton lint and yarn increases relative to the baseline, and its exports expand. There is a delayed response in the domestic textile sector. Initially the effects are positive but minimal in 2008, as the industry competes with the export of cotton lint and yarn for its inputs. Then, as capital accumulates in the textile sector, its output improves and converges after about four years toward the increase in raw cotton and cotton lint and yarn production over the baseline.

There is an increase in real income over time from a TFP improvement in raw cotton. Differential effects across household groups are largely due to dynamic interactions across the cotton-related sectors and the rest of the economy. Farmers' wages, returns to land, and returns to capital in agriculture initially decline relative to the baseline values, and the incomes of large and medium farmers, small farmers, and agricultural workers fall. However, as the other sectors adjust over time, all factor prices improve from the baseline, leading to higher incomes for all households.

An improvement in TFP in both raw cotton and cotton lint and yarn initially increases the output of both sectors relative to the baseline, with prices for the output of both sectors declining. With the TFP of cotton lint and yarn increased, the level of output of raw cotton rises more than in the previous scenario, and farm incomes suffer less initial decline and a shorter adjustment to higher levels. With lower raw cotton input costs and the reduction in the cost of producing cotton lint and yarn resulting from its improved TFP, the export competitiveness of the sector initially surges relative to the baseline. Again the initial effects on the textile sector are positive but minimal. A period of dynamic adjustment occurs through 2012, then over the long run output converges across the three sectors to a level about 3.5 percent higher than the baseline.

The most positive scenario involves higher productivity in all three cotton-related sectors. There is an immediate and sustained improvement in each sector's output compared with the baseline. Reduction in their cost of production makes both the cotton lint and yarn and textile sectors more competitive in the export market, with a sustained increase over the long run in exports of these sectors compared with the baseline. Factor prices and household incomes improve the most in this scenario, with the least adjustment costs.

Overall the results of simulations 1 and 2 demonstrate the different effects arising from two largely external positive shocks—the increase in foreign savings strengthens the currency and creates a boom in the non-trade sectors, whereas an increase in world cotton and textile prices improves Pakistan's terms of trade and generates a boom in the cotton and textile sectors in particular. An inflow of foreign savings depresses traded sectors but stimulates a boom in investment and nontraded goods. Because these cotton-related sectors represent such a large share of overall exports, an export boom in these sectors also strengthens the currency, and this result negatively affects other tradables and foreign remittances to households. These different effects need to be understood by policymakers trying to assess, for example, the performance of the yarn and textile sectors under more liberalized trade rules, but also in light of the capital inflow and increasing foreign remittances. Simulations 3 and 4 are relevant to policymakers who must direct limited domestic resources to capacity-building public investments but who also face calls for more direct support from industry lobbies. The dynamic analysis of TFP improvements highlights the desirability of simultaneous efforts to remove constraints to production across these closely related sectors.

CHAPTER 2

The International Cotton Market

This chapter presents broad trends in production, consumption, trade, and prices in the international market for cotton, textiles, and apparel; it also highlights factors behind the movements in the international price of cotton as well as major players in the market, including Pakistan and India.

Trends in Cotton Production, Consumption, and Trade

The total global area devoted to cotton production hardly changed over the period 1965–2006. Its average annual growth is 0.1 percent (Table 2.1). However, productivity in terms of yield (kilograms per hectare) improved by an average of 1.8 percent annually. Thus the average output growth of 1.9 percent was largely due to improvements in yield.

International trade is a major component of the cotton market. However, while exports and imports of cotton grew relatively faster (average annual rates of 2.5 and 2.4 percent, respectively) than production and consumption (average rates of 1.9 and 2 percent, respectively) over the period 1965–2006, the export-to-production ratio exhibits a declining trend after the mid-1970s, when it reached a peak of nearly 50 percent (Figure 2.1).

The largest producer of cotton is China, which accounts for about a quarter of world production (Table 2.2). Historically the United States has long been the second major producer of cotton, but as of 2006 it was surpassed by India. Over the past 35 years, the average annual growth of cotton production in India has been 4.6 percent. Yet since 2000 cotton production in India has been growing rapidly, at an average annual rate of 11.6 percent. The surge in cotton production in India is mainly due to the introduction of Bt (*Bacillus thuringiensis*) cotton in 2002.[1] On the other hand, over the same period, the average annual growth in cotton production in Pakistan was 3.7 percent. This relatively high growth has enabled Pakistan to double its share of the overall world production of cotton. At present it is the fourth major producer in the world.

Table 2.3 presents data on harvested area and yield for the four major cotton producers. Except for variability around a flat trend, there has not been much change in area in either China or the United States. But there have been some noticeable increases in India and Pakistan. The yield in China and the United States is higher than the world average, and that in India and Pakistan is lower. Yet there has been some improvement. Over the period 1970–2006, while the improvement in world yield was 76 percent, that in China was 149 percent; in India, 193

[1]Bt cotton contains a gene, derived from the soil bacterium that gives the plant its name, which protects the cotton plant against bollworms by producing a special protein. Bollworms feeding on Bt cotton leaves become sleepy and lethargic, causing less damage to the crop.

percent; and in Pakistan, 101 percent. The improvement in yield for the United States over the period was 66 percent.

The major source of world cotton exports is the United States (Table 2.4). From an average of 17.8 percent in 1970–74, its share of world exports increased to 36 percent in 2000–03. In 2004 the share improved to 41.2 percent, but it declined slightly to 39.4 percent in 2007. The former Soviet Union accounted for a large proportion of cotton exports in the 1970s, but its share has dropped significantly, especially in the first half of the 2000s. Exports from the African region have improved through the years, and the same is true of Australia, except in some recent years. Cotton exports from China, India, and Pakistan are relatively limited, although there is substantial annual variability in these countries' exports.

Consumption of cotton is determined largely by the size of a country's textile industries. China, the world's leading producer of textiles, is also the major user of cotton. At present it consumes more than a third of world production (Table 2.5). India

Table 2.1 World cotton supply and use, selected years, 1965–2006

	Supply					Use (million 480-lb bales)		
Year beginning August 1	Harvested area (million ha)	Yield (kg/ha)	Beginning stocks (million 480-lb bales)	Production	Imports	Consumption	Exports	Ending stocks
1965	33.3	372.5	29.0	56.9	17.4	53.8	17.0	32.6
1970	31.8	380.5	22.4	55.6	24.6	57.1	23.6	21.8
1975	29.9	393.4	33.4	54.0	26.1	61.6	26.0	25.9
1980	32.4	426.3	21.2	63.4	27.3	65.0	26.3	20.6
1985	31.6	552.5	42.1	80.2	28.7	75.3	28.1	47.6
1990	33.2	572.2	25.0	87.1	30.4	85.5	29.6	27.4
1991	34.8	596.5	27.4	95.3	28.7	86.2	28.2	37.0
1992	32.6	549.0	37.0	82.3	27.0	86.3	25.5	34.4
1993	30.7	550.5	34.4	77.6	27.8	85.6	26.7	27.7
1994	32.2	583.2	27.7	86.3	30.6	84.5	28.2	31.9
1995	36.0	567.2	31.9	93.7	27.4	85.8	27.4	39.9
1996	33.7	580.9	39.9	90.0	29.0	87.8	26.9	44.3
1997	33.8	594.6	44.3	92.2	26.3	87.3	26.7	48.8
1998	32.9	565.9	48.8	85.5	25.3	84.8	23.5	51.3
1999	32.3	591.8	51.3	87.7	28.4	91.1	27.2	49.2
2000	32.0	604.0	49.2	88.9	27.3	92.2	26.4	46.8
2001	33.7	637.4	46.8	98.8	29.9	94.3	29.0	52.1
2002	30.4	631.0	52.1	88.3	30.6	98.3	30.3	42.3
2003	32.1	646.0	45.4	95.3	34.8	98.1	33.2	44.3
2004	35.8	742.9	44.3	122.1	34.6	108.7	35.0	57.4
2005	34.9	734.5	57.4	117.7	45.9	116.0	44.5	60.4
2006	34.7	765.1	60.4	121.9	—	123.3	—	—
Average growth[a]	0.1	1.8	1.8	1.9	2.5	2.0	2.4	1.6

Source: Economic Research Service, USDA (2007).

[a]1965–2006 geometric growth (percent); 1965–2005 for imports, exports, and ending stocks.

Figure 2.1 Trade ratio: Exports/production (percent)

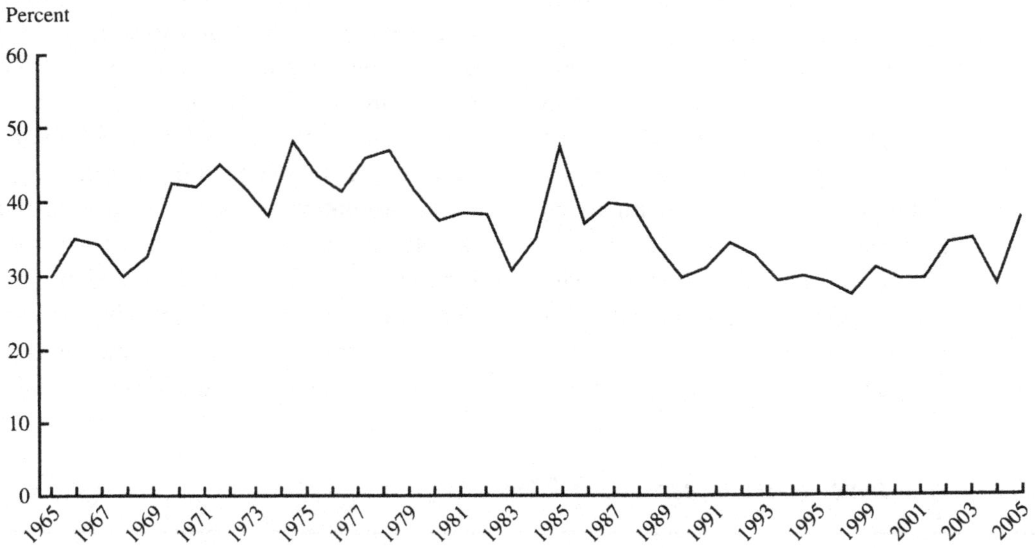

Source: Economic Research Service, USDA (2007).

Table 2.2 Major sources of world cotton production, 1970–2007 (percent share)

Period average	China	United States	India	Pakistan	Brazil	Former Soviet Union	Turkey	Others
1970–74	17.3	19.4	8.5	4.8	4.6	18.4	3.9	23.1
1975–79	16.8	19.4	9.3	4.1	4.0	20.4	3.8	22.2
1980–84	25.7	16.9	9.6	4.9	4.5	16.0	3.4	18.9
1985–89	23.1	16.5	10.7	8.0	4.3	15.6	3.3	18.7
1990–94	24.3	19.9	11.8	8.6	3.0	11.7	3.3	17.4
1995–99	22.4	19.2	14.4	8.4	2.4	8.0	4.2	21.1
2000–03	24.1	19.6	13.4	8.8	4.8	7.2	4.1	17.9
2004	25.4	19.0	15.6	9.1	4.8	6.6	3.4	16.1
2005	25.1	20.3	16.2	8.6	4.0	7.1	3.0	15.7
2006[a]	29.1	17.7	17.9	8.1	5.7	6.7	3.2	11.5
2007[b]	29.7	15.8	19.7	8.2	5.9	6.9	2.8	11.0
Average growth[c]	3.3	1.7	4.6	3.7	2.6	–0.7	1.6	0.1

Source: Economic Research Service, USDA (2007).
[a]Estimates.
[b]Forecast.
[c]1970–2007 geometric growth of volume of production (percent).

Table 2.3 Harvested cotton area and yield, 1970–2006

Period average	World: Harvested area (million ha)	World: Yield (kg/ha)	China: Harvested area (million ha)	China: Yield (kg/ha)	United States: Harvested area (million ha)	United States: Yield (kg/ha)	India: Harvested area (million ha)	India: Yield (kg/ha)	Pakistan: Harvested area (million ha)	Pakistan: Yield (kg/ha)
1970–74	33	400	5	459	5	527	8	147	2	330
1975–79	32	409	5	451	5	540	8	158	2	281
1980–84	32	476	6	680	4	594	8	190	2	343
1985–89	31	548	5	797	4	701	7	257	3	548
1990–94	33	570	6	773	5	741	8	288	3	594
1995–99	34	580	5	966	5	707	9	311	3	569
2000–01	33	622	4	1,096	5	751	9	292	3	601
2002–06	34	704	5	1,141	5	875	8	431	3	666
Average 1970–2006	—	532	—	771	—	674	—	257	—	480
Average growth (%)[a]	—	76	—	149	—	66	—	193	—	101

Source: Economic Research Service, USDA (2007).
[a]Between two subperiods: 1970–74 and 2002–06 (percent).

Table 2.4 Major exporters of cotton, 1970–2007 (percent share)

Period average	China	United States	India	Pakistan	Brazil	Former Soviet Union	Africa[a]	Australia	Others
1970–74	0.5	17.8	0.6	2.9	3.7	37.3	2.4	0.1	34.7
1975–79	0.4	21.1	0.7	1.7	0.6	41.3	2.9	0.4	30.9
1980–84	1.4	23.6	1.4	4.2	1.3	38.4	3.5	1.8	24.5
1985–89	7.0	18.4	1.6	8.7	1.5	34.5	5.7	3.7	18.9
1990–94	2.3	25.9	1.8	3.6	0.8	32.6	8.0	6.0	19.0
1995–99	1.9	25.0	1.7	1.7	0.1	22.9	13.0	9.8	23.9
2000–03	1.5	36.0	0.7	1.0	2.0	17.6	12.6	10.2	18.3
2004	0.1	41.2	1.9	1.6	4.4	17.0	11.8	5.7	16.3
2005	0.1	39.4	7.8	0.6	4.4	16.3	10.0	6.5	14.9
2006[b]	0.2	34.6	13.5	0.7	3.5	18.3	10.1	5.7	13.5
2007[c]	0.1	39.4	12.2	0.6	6.8	16.8	7.4	3.5	13.1

Source: Economic Research Service, USDA (2007).
[a]Includes Benin, Burkina Faso, Cameroon, Central African Republic, Chad, Ivory Coast, Mali, Niger, Senegal, and Togo.
[b]Estimates.
[c]Forecast.

Table 2.5 Major users of cotton, 1970–2007 (percent share)

Period average	China	United States	India	Pakistan	Brazil	Former Soviet Union	Turkey	Others
1970–74	19	13	9	4	3	15	2	37
1975–79	20	11	9	3	4	14	2	37
1980–84	24	8	9	3	4	12	2	36
1985–89	24	9	10	4	4	11	3	35
1990–94	24	12	11	8	4	7	4	31
1995–99	23	12	15	8	4	3	6	29
2000–03	29	19	14	9	4	4	6	14
2004	35	19	14	10	4	3	7	8
2005	39	20	14	10	4	3	6	4
2006[a]	41	15	15	10	4	3	6	8
2007[b]	43	16	15	10	3	3	6	5

Source: Economic Research Service, USDA (2007).
[a]Estimates.
[b]Forecast.

Table 2.6 Major importers of cotton, 1970–2006 (percent share)

Period average	China	United States	India	Pakistan	Brazil	Former Soviet Union	Russia	EU-25	Japan	Indo-nesia	South Korea	Thai-land	Taiwan	Others
1970–74	4.4	0.2	1.6	0.0	0.0	28.2	0.0	28.6	14.2	0.9	2.4	1.1	2.8	15.7
1975–79	6.7	0.1	0.8	0.0	0.0	27.9	0.0	25.2	11.9	1.4	3.8	1.5	3.7	17.1
1980–84	5.7	0.1	0.0	0.2	0.1	25.6	0.0	25.7	12.4	2.0	3.8	1.7	4.2	18.5
1985–89	2.1	0.0	0.2	0.0	1.1	25.0	10.8	25.1	10.7	3.2	3.2	3.4	5.5	9.8
1990–94	6.0	0.0	0.7	0.7	4.5	15.7	11.7	21.2	8.0	6.6	3.5	5.4	4.6	11.3
1995–99	6.2	1.0	1.7	1.4	6.5	6.0	4.2	19.8	5.0	7.8	3.7	5.2	4.9	26.5
2000–02	4.2	0.1	5.9	2.6	1.6	7.0	5.8	15.0	3.7	8.3	3.5	6.1	4.3	31.9
2003	25.3	0.1	2.3	5.2	1.6	5.0	4.2	9.5	2.2	6.2	3.7	4.8	2.9	27.0
2004	18.5	0.1	3.0	5.1	0.6	4.9	4.2	9.3	2.4	6.4	3.9	6.6	3.9	31.4
2005	42.0	0.1	0.9	3.5	0.7	4.0	3.1	5.3	1.4	4.8	2.2	4.1	2.5	25.5
2006	26.8	0.0	1.0	5.8	1.3	4.8	3.6	5.4	1.5	5.6	2.7	4.9	2.9	33.4

Source: Economic Research Service, USDA (2007).

Figure 2.2 Cotton price: COTLOOK A and B indexes and U.S. price

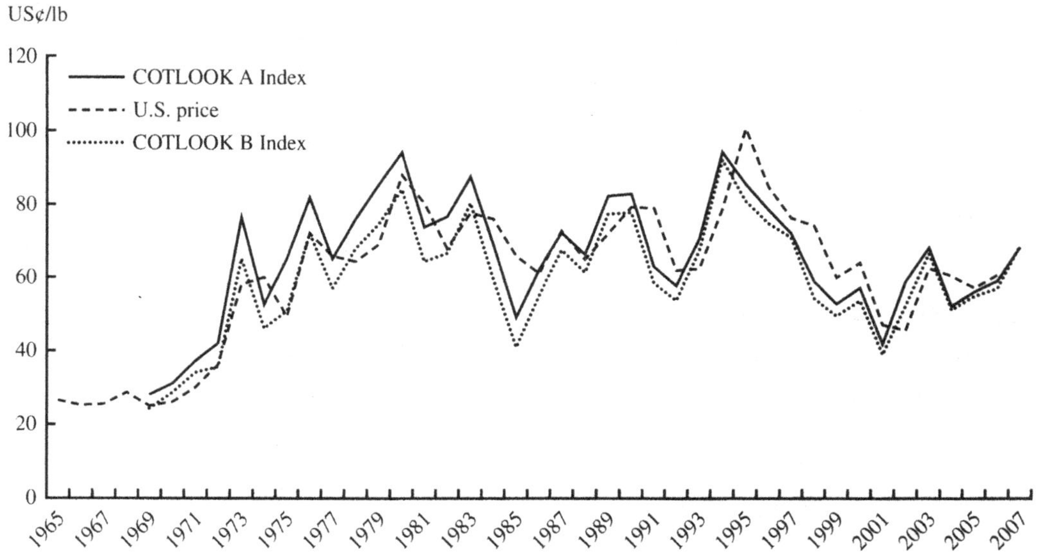

Source: ICAC (2007).

and Pakistan have increasingly become major users of cotton as well, owing to their relatively larger textile industries.

There are some years when domestic cotton production in China does not match domestic consumption, forcing the Chinese textile industry to rely on imports. Cotton imports into China were significant in the mid-1990s and in the first half of the present decade (Table 2.6). Cotton imports into the former Soviet Union, the EU-25, and Japan dropped steadily over time, while those into Indonesia and Thailand increased.[2] Cotton imports into both India and Pakistan have increased over the past 10 years.

Trends in International Cotton Prices

Three indicators of international cotton prices, the COTLOOK A and COTLOOK B indexes and the U.S. price, are presented in Figure 2.2.[3] Together these indexes generally move in the same direction. The COTLOOK A index is generally higher than the COTLOOK B index, while the U.S. price index is either below or above the two others. Cotton from Pakistan is grouped within the COTLOOK B index.

There is a high degree of variability in the international price of cotton. While an increasing trend in nominal prices was observed from the second half of the 1960s through the 1970s, there was no clear direction in the 1980s. The early 1990s saw a sharp hike in cotton prices until 1994, then a significant drop was observed in the second half of the 1990s until 2001. During these years, international cotton prices (the A and B indexes) fell nearly 60 percent, while U.S. cotton prices fell 40 percent. Wide swings in cotton prices have continued since 2002.

[2] The members of the EU-25 are Austria, Belgium, Cyprus, the Czech Republic, Denmark, Estonia, Finland, France, Germany, Greece, Hungary, Ireland, Italy, Latvia, Lithuania, Luxembourg, Malta, the Netherlands, Poland, Portugal, Slovakia, Slovenia, Spain, Sweden, and the United Kingdom.

[3] The COTLOOK A index is the average of the five lowest quotations of 16 styles of cotton (middling 1$^{3}/_{32}$ in.) traded in North European ports from the following origins: Australia, Brazil, China, Francophone Africa, Greece, India, Mexico, Pakistan, Paraguay, Spain, Syria, Tanzania, Turkey, the United States, and Uzbekistan. The COTLOOK B index is the average of the three lowest quotations of eight styles of coarser grades of cotton from Argentina, Brazil, China, India, Pakistan, Turkey, the United States, and Uzbekistan.

After a recovery in 2002 and 2003, prices dropped in 2004. The past three years have seen improvement in cotton prices. Along with the increase in world food and oil prices, there has been a sustained increase in world cotton prices, amounting to 5.4 percent in 2006, 9.1 percent in 2007, and 26.9 percent in the first eight months of 2008.

Factors Influencing International Cotton Prices

Short-term fluctuations in the international price of cotton are the result of various factors, such as expectations, production, and inventories. For example, natural calamities coupled with a significant drop in stocks in China resulted in a sharp increase in prices in 2003. Lower than expected consumption and the expected bumper crop resulted in a decline in the domestic price in 2004 (FAO 2006).

Over the long term, international cotton prices are affected by improvements in yield due to improved inputs, such as expanded use of irrigation, fertilizers, and chemicals. Other technological developments that reduce the cost of production, such as the introduction of genetically modified varieties, also affect prices. Competition from substitute fibers and trade-distorting policy shifts in major cotton-producing and exporting countries also affect international prices.

One recent development in cotton production has been the focus on cost reduction through less-intensive use of chemicals (Baffes 2004). Contributing to this development has been the introduction of genetically modified seed technology. The technological developments of the 1990s that resulted in the introduction of Bt cotton present the potential for reducing cost and thereby increasing profitability. The leading cotton-producing countries that have introduced this technology include China, India, and Mexico in the Northern Hemisphere, and Argentina, Australia, and South Africa in the Southern Hemisphere. Brazil, Indonesia, Israel, Pakistan, and Turkey are presently in the trial stage.[4] However, the largest user of Bt cotton is the United States, where it is estimated that 70 percent of the available cotton area was sown with genetically modified varieties in the 2003/04 season. In Australia 44 percent of the cotton area was sown to such varieties in the 2002/03 season. In China more than 20 million hectares were planted with such varieties in 2002. At present it is estimated that 22 percent of the world's cotton planting involves genetically modified varieties, up from 2 percent in 1996/97 (Baffes 2004).

Synthetic fibers such as rayon and polyester are substitutes for cotton fibers. Since the early 1990s, there have been major structural shifts in the production of cotton and polyester fibers (Figure 2.3). In the 1980s cotton and polyester shares were each around 50 percent of total fiber production. From 1992 onward the share of polyester improved to about 60 percent, while that of cotton dropped to about 40 percent. The synthetic/cotton price ratio does not appear to be the main factor behind the shift in consumption. Over the past two decades the two prices generally move in the same direction. One of the most likely reasons for the shift is the durability of clothing based on polyester (or polyester mixed with cotton) compared with clothing made of pure cotton.

In the early 1990s Townsend and Gutichounts (1994) estimated that about two-thirds of world cotton production took place in countries that implemented some form of trade-distorting government policies, such as taxes and subsidies. Recently the International Cotton Advisory Committee (ICAC) found that eight countries provided direct support to cotton production: Brazil, China, Egypt, Greece, Mexico, Spain, Turkey, and the United States (Table 2.7). By far the largest amount

[4]In Pakistan the Ministry of Food, Agriculture, and Livestock announced plans on January 5, 2007, to release the first home-grown insect-resistant variety of Bt cotton (*Dawn* the Internet Edition 2007).

Figure 2.3 Cotton versus polyester fibers

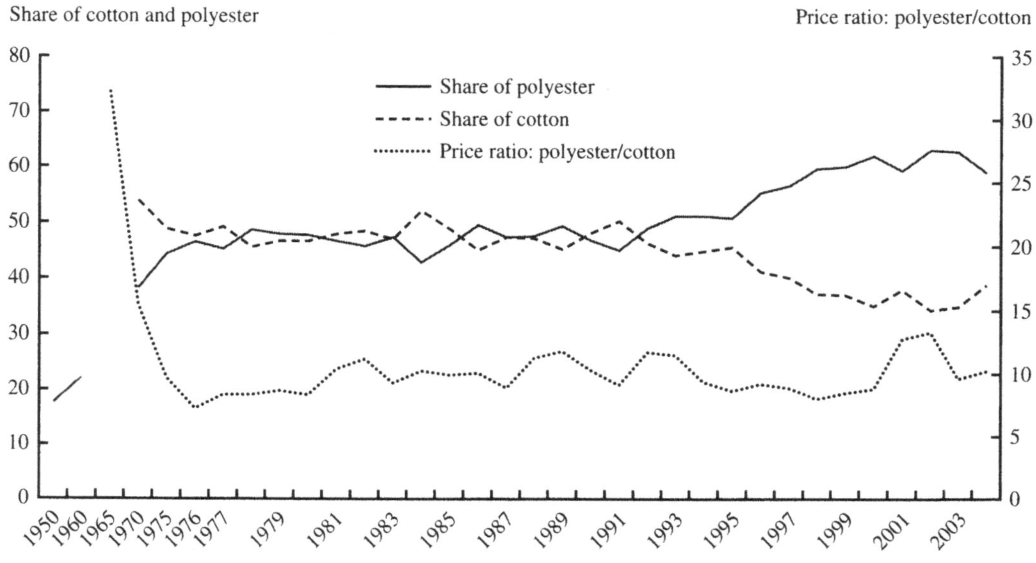

Source: ICAC (2007).

of direct government assistance to cotton producers is provided in the United States, where it reached nearly $4 billion in 2001/02. The U.S. government support is offered through various policy instruments (Table 2.8).

A number of studies have attempted to quantify the impact of government support on world prices and production, particularly focusing on the period 1994–2002, when prices dropped sharply. Orden et al. (2008) and the Food and Agriculture Organization of the United Nations (FAO 2004) surveyed those studies and found that, generally, the elimination of subsidies is likely to improve international cotton prices. However, the magnitude of the impact depends on the method used to assess it, such as a computable general equilibrium model, a partial equilibrium model, or econometric estimates of supply response.

To cite some conclusions from individual studies, the estimates of the Overseas Development Institute (Gillson et al. 2004) indicate that, if the cotton market were to be liberalized, production in the United States and the European Union (EU) would fall and world cotton prices would increase by between 18 and 28 percent. This change would in turn increase the export earnings of all developing countries by $610 million. West and Central African countries could gain between $94 million and $355 million in earnings from cotton production. ICAC (2003) finds that the removal of subsidies will result in lower production in the countries concerned, and world cotton prices will therefore increase by 21 percent in 2000–01 and 73 percent in 2001–02.

According to Goreaux (2003) the export earnings of West and Central Africa were reduced by $250 million because of cotton support policies. The removal of subsidies is estimated to increase world cotton prices by 18 percent. The study by Reeves et al. (2001) finds that the removal of production and export subsidies by the United States and the EU could lead to a 20 percent reduction in U.S. cotton production and a 50 percent fall in U.S. cotton exports. This in turn could increase prices by 10.7 percent from the observed benchmark. The study carried out by the Centre for International Economics (CIE 2001) indicates that the removal of subsidies would increase world cotton prices by 10.7 percent. Sum-

Table 2.7 Direct government assistance to cotton producers, 1997–2003 (million US$)

Country	1997–98	1998–99	1999–2000	2000–01	2001–02	2002–03
United States	1,163	1,946	3,432	2,148	3,964	2,620
China	2,013	2,648	1,534	1,900	1,196	750
Greece	659	660	596	537	735	718
Spain	211	204	199	179	245	239
Turkey	—	220	199	106	59	57
Brazil	29	52	44	44	10	0
Mexico	13	15	28	23	18	7
Egypt	290	—	20	14	23	33

Sources: ICAC (2002, 2003), U.S. Department of Agriculture, and European Union.
Note: — means not available.

Table 2.8 Government assistance to U.S. cotton producers, 1995–2003 (million US$)

Policy instruments	1995–96	1996–97	1997–98	1998–99	1999–2000	2000–01	2001–02	2002–03
Coupled payments	3	—	28	535	1,613	563	2,507	248
Production flexibility contracts/ direct payments	—	599	597	637	614	575	474	914
Emergency/counter-cyclical payments	—	—	—	316	613	613	524	1,264
Insurance	180	157	148	151	170	162	236	194
Step-2	34	3	390	308	422	236	196	—
Total	217	759	1,163	1,947	3,432	2,149	3,937	2,620

Sources: U.S. Department of Agriculture (assistance) and International Cotton Advisory Committee (production).
Note: — means not available.

ner (2003) finds that, without U.S. subsidies for cotton during 1999–2002, world cotton prices would have been higher by 13 percent. At the lower end of estimates, Tokarick (2003) finds that multilateral trade liberalization across cotton and other agricultural markets will improve cotton prices by only 2.8 percent, while Poonyth et al. (2004) calculate that the improvement in cotton prices would range between 3.1 and 4.8 percent.

From these studies it is clear that the impact of trade-distorting policies in major producing and exporting countries on world cotton prices is significant, with many estimates in the range of 10–20 percent. This outcome would have far-reaching effects on rural farm households, especially in cotton-producing developing countries. Estimates from FAO (2004) indicate that as many as 100 million rural households may have been directly or indirectly involved in cotton production.

Prices of Cotton Yarn and Cotton Fabric

Cotton is processed into yarn and then fabric, and these commodities are also heavily traded internationally. There are no readily available price indexes for cotton yarn and cotton fabric comparable to the COTLOOK A and B indexes. To provide an idea of how world prices of cotton yarn and fabric move with world cotton prices, we derived traded-price indexes for these cotton products using data from the United Nations Commodity Trade Statistics database (United Nations Statistics Division 2006). We selected major world exporters of cotton yarn and tracked their data on value and quantity traded from 1990 to 2005. Similarly we tracked the data on value and quantity traded for major exporters of cotton fabric. Price series were computed for these products and are expressed, including COTLOOK B, in Table 2.9. For the period 1990–2005, the coefficient of variation of COTLOOK B is 22.9 percent, while that for cotton yarn is 13.0 percent and that for cotton fabric is 7.7 percent. Figure 2.4 shows that COTLOOK B is more volatile

Table 2.9 World prices of cotton, cotton yarn, and cotton fabric, 1990–2005

Year	Cotton[a]	Cotton yarn[b]	Cotton fabric[c]
1990	144.9	100.8	125.8
1991	108.9	104.3	124.3
1992	100.0	116.6	111.7
1993	125.3	106.4	99.8
1994	171.9	123.4	107.0
1995	150.9	136.8	121.7
1996	139.4	125.8	124.2
1997	132.2	116.9	115.0
1998	101.1	111.7	113.3
1999	92.3	105.1	106.9
2000	100.0	100.0	100.0
2001	72.5	89.5	100.2
2002	97.6	83.8	116.0
2003	124.1	97.5	111.1
2004	95.3	101.9	118.4
2005	95.3	94.9	116.9
Mean	115.7	107.2	113.3
Standard deviation	26.5	14.0	8.7
Coefficient of variation (%)	22.9	13.0	7.7
1994–2001 change (%)	-57.8	-27.4	-6.4
Ratio[d]	—	0.47	0.23

Sources: United Nations Commodity Trade Statistics and International Cotton Advisory Committee.
Note: Values are expressed as an index, with the year 2000 as the base.
[a]Cotton is per COTLOOK-B (see text for explanation).
[b]Cotton yarn is item 6513 under the Standard International Trade Classification (SITC) Revision 3. Countries include China, China–Hong Kong Special Administrative Region, India, Italy, Pakistan, and United States.
[c]Cotton fabric, woven, is item 652 under the SITC Revision 3. Countries: Belgium, China, France, Germany, India, Hong Kong, Italy, Japan, Republic of Korea, Netherlands, Pakistan, United States, and United Kingdom.
[d]For cotton yarn: change in the price of cotton yarn over change in the price of COTLOOK-B; for cotton fabric: change in the price of cotton fabric over change in the price of cotton yarn.

Figure 2.4 World prices of cotton, cotton yarn, and cotton fabric

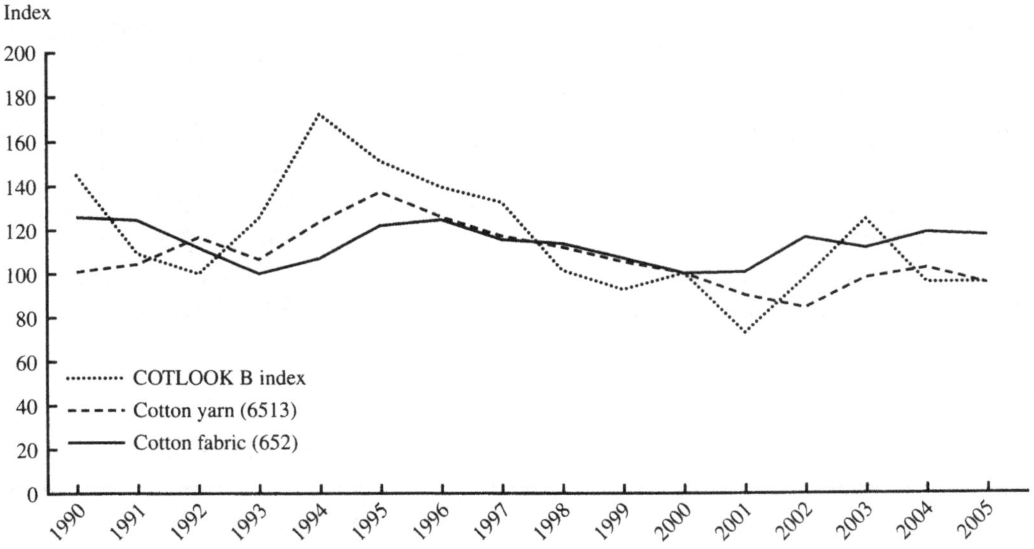

Sources: ICAC (2003) and World Trade Organization (2007).

compared to cotton yarn prices and cotton fabric prices.

The period 1994–2001 saw a drop of 57.8 percent in COTLOOK B. Over this period, the price of cotton yarn dropped by 27.4 percent and by 38.8 percent from lagged peak-to-trough yarn prices in 1995–2002. The drop in the price of cotton fabric was not as dramatic, at 6.4 percent over the period 1994–2001 and 19.4 percent from the peak textile prices in 1996. Using these reduced-form relationships, the "elasticity" between COTLOOK B and the price of cotton yarn during the period 1994–2001 is 0.47, and that between the price of cotton yarn and the price of cotton fabric is 0.23.

Global Trends in the Markets for Textiles and Clothing

This section presents trends in the world markets for textiles and clothing, the position of Pakistan and India in these markets, and some information on Pakistan's world exports of textiles and the sources of its imports.

In 2005 the world market for textiles totaled $203 billion (Table 2.10). It has grown strongly in the past 15 years. In the 1990s the average annual growth of the market was about 5 percent. In 2003 and 2004 its annual growth was more than 10 percent, slowing in 2005 to 3.9 percent.

The European Union (EU-25) accounts for a third of the total world exports of textiles. This is mainly intra-EU trade. The EU's textile trade with the rest of the world accounts for less than 12 percent of the total. China has a rapidly growing share of the world textile market. In 1990 China accounted for 6.9 percent of world textile exports. Its exports surged after 2000. By 2005 China's share of the world market was 20.2 percent. The shares of the other major producers of textiles are generally stable, implying falling shares for numerous other countries. Hong Kong's share, which is mostly due to re-exporting, is about 7 percent, with about the same level for the United States. The share for India in 2005 was about 4 percent, and that for Pakistan was about 3.5 percent.

Table 2.11 presents the structure of the world market for clothing. In 2005 total world exports of clothing amounted to $275.6 billion, somewhat larger than the world mar-

Table 2.10 Textile exports of selected economies, selected years, 1990–2005

	1990	2000	2003	2004	2005
World exports (billion US$)	104.4	157.1	173.7	195.4	203.0
World average annual growth (%)	—	5.1	10.6	12.5	3.9
		Share of world exports (%)			
EU-25	—	35.9	37.4	37.0	33.5
Intra-exports	—	24.9	25.2	24.5	21.9
Extra-exports	—	14.7	9.7	7.4	11.6
China	6.9	10.3	15.5	17.1	20.2
Hong Kong	7.9	8.6	7.5	7.3	6.8
Re-exports	5.8	7.8	7.1	7.0	6.5
United States	4.8	7.0	6.3	6.1	6.1
Republic of Korea	5.8	8.1	6.2	5.5	5.1
Taipei, China	5.9	7.6	5.4	5.1	4.8
India	2.1	3.8	3.9	3.6	3.9
Pakistan	2.6	2.9	3.5	3.1	3.5
Turkey	1.4	2.3	3.0	3.3	3.5
Japan	5.6	4.5	3.7	3.7	3.4
Indonesia	1.2	2.2	1.7	1.6	1.7

Source: World Trade Organization (2007).
Note: Textiles are item 65 under the SITC Revision 3.

ket for textiles. The market is also growing strongly, with an average growth rate of 8.3 percent in the 1990s, rising to 17.6 percent in 2003 and 11.4 percent in 2004, and then slowing to 6.4 percent in 2005.

Similar to the structure of the world market for textiles, the EU has the largest share in the world market for clothing, and again this is mostly intra-EU trade. There has been remarkable growth in China's exports of clothing, with its share of the world market increasing from 8.9 percent in 1990 to 26.9 percent in 2005. India's share is stable at about 3 percent. Pakistan's share is also stable at about 1 percent.

Liberalization of International Trade in Textiles and Clothing

During the past 30 years there have been three major shifts in the rules that govern the international trade in textiles and clothing. From 1974 to 1994, the rules set forth in the MFA provided the parameters for bilateral negotiations on how quotas for trade in textiles and clothing would be determined. Under the MFA discriminatory quotas were allowed in areas where the increase in imports had the potential to cause domestic market disruptions. Austria, Canada, the EU, Finland, Norway, and the United States applied quotas exclusively to exports from developing countries.

With the advent of the World Trade Organization (WTO) in 1995, the MFA was replaced by the WTO Agreement on Textiles and Clothing (ATC), which was designed to provide a transitional phase between the MFA and full integration of the textile and clothing industry into the multilateral trading system. Under the ATC, Canada, the EU, Norway, and the United States retained some quota restrictions until

Table 2.11 Clothing exports of selected economies, selected years, 1990–2005

	1990	2000	2003	2004	2005
World exports (billion US$)	108.1	197.8	232.6	259.1	275.6
World average annual growth (%)	—	8.3	17.6	11.4	6.4
		Share of world exports (%)			
EU-25	—	26.9	29.4	29.7	29.2
Intra-exports	—	20.1	22.0	2.2	20.9
Extra-exports	—	6.8	7.4	7.4	8.2
China	8.9	18.2	22.4	23.9	26.9
Hong Kong	14.2	12.2	10.1	9.7	9.9
Re-exports	5.7	7.2	6.4	6.5	7.3
Turkey	3.1	3.3	4.3	4.3	4.3
India	2.3	3.1	2.8	2.6	3.0
Mexico	0.5	4.4	3.2	2.9	2.6
Bangladesh	0.6	2.0	2.1	2.2	2.3
Indonesia	1.5	2.4	1.8	1.7	1.9
United States	2.4	4.4	2.4	2.0	1.8
Romania	0.3	1.2	1.7	1.8	1.7
Thailand	2.6	1.9	1.6	1.5	1.5
Pakistan	0.9	1.1	1.2	1.2	1.3
Sri Lanka	0.6	1.4	1.1	1.1	1.0
Republic of Korea	7.3	2.5	1.6	1.3	0.9
Malaysia	1.2	1.1	0.9	0.9	0.9
Philippines	1.6	1.3	1.0	0.8	0.8

Source: World Trade Organization (2007).
Note: Clothing is item 84 under the SITC Revision 3.

January 1, 2005, when the quotas for trade in textiles and clothing were lifted and replaced by tariffs alone.

Prior to the lifting of quotas, a number of studies estimated the potential effects of liberalized international trade in textiles and clothing. To cite a few of these studies, Nordias (2004) argued that China and India would come to dominate world trade. The share for China alone was predicted to reach more than 50 percent during the post-ATC period. Tables 2.10 and 2.11 indicate the rapid increase in China's share of the world market in both textiles and clothing. But India's share of the world market has not shown significant enlargement so far.

Martin (2004) examined the possible effects of quota elimination on Pakistan. He argues that improvement in productivity is the key issue if Pakistan is to increase its share of the world markets. This is because the international markets will be more price responsive after the abolition of quotas. This will present opportunities for suppliers with high productivity, while less competitive suppliers can expect to suffer losses in market share. Thus, for Pakistan, Martin (2004, ii) concludes that "raising productivity—either by improving the ef-

Table 2.12 Pakistan exports of textiles and clothing to restricted markets, selected years, 1990–2006 (percent)

Year	Textile fibers[a]	Textile yarn, fabric, etc.[b]	Clothing and accessories[c]	Combined[d]
1990	28.9	43.9	88.4	52.9
1995	22.4	37.6	89.9	50.8
2000	24.9	49.6	90.1	61.4
2002	34.4	54.5	84.5	63.6
2004	16.1	55.9	86.7	65.1
2005	19.8	63.7	85.1	70.1
2006	20.7	58.7	88.7	68.6

Source: United Nations Commodity Trade Statistics.
Note: Restricted markets include Canada, the European Union, Norway, and the United States.
[a]Textile fibers are item 26 under the SITC Revision 3. This is the ratio of Pakistan exports of textile fibers to these markets to overall Pakistan exports of textile fibers.
[b]Textile yarn, fabric, etc., is item 65 under the SITC Revision 3. This is the ratio of Pakistan exports of textile yarn, fabric, etc., to these markets to overall Pakistan exports of textile yarn, fabric, etc.
[c]Clothing and accessories are item 84 under the SITC Revision 3. This is the ratio of Pakistan exports of clothing and accessories to these markets to overall Pakistan exports of clothing and accessories.
[d]The combined value is the ratio of Pakistan exports of fibers, textiles, and clothing to these markets to overall Pakistan exports of fibers, textiles, and clothing.

ficiency of the production process or [by improving] the range and the quality of the products produced—is key to reaping the benefit from the abolition of the MFA."

Even with the abolition of the MFA, Pakistan's exports of textile yarn, fabric, and other commodities that go to the restricted markets have not declined relative to its overall exports of these items. According to the data presented in Table 2.12, the share of Pakistan's exports of textile fibers that go to Canada, the EU, Norway, and the United States has declined from 34.4 percent in 2002 to 20.7 percent in 2006. This decrease is due to Pakistan's efforts to increase value added by processing fibers into yarn, fabric, garments, and textile made-ups, as discussed in the next chapter.[5] However, the shares of "textile yarn, fabric, etc." and "clothing and accessories" remain high. The combined ratio increased from 52.9 percent in 1990 to 70.1 percent in 2005 and 68.6 percent in 2006, indicating that Pakistan remains particularly competitive in some specific textile product lines.

[5]*Made-ups* is the textile-industry term for such products as cushion covers, kitchen linens, and rugs and mats.

CHAPTER 3

The Cotton-Textile Industry in Pakistan

This chapter describes the structure of the cotton, textile, and apparel industries in Pakistan. The first stage of the process is the production of raw cotton, which is classified as agriculture. Next comes ginning, during which cotton lint and cotton fibers are produced. The textile industry is considered to start at the spinning stage, during which cotton fibers are spun into yarn. Yarn is weaved into fabrics. Fabrics, in various forms, are used in the making of apparel, clothing, and garments and in the production of textile made-ups, such as towels or bedwear. In each of these stages, output is either exported to the international market or sold domestically, either to other sectors for further processing or to the household sector for final consumption. There have been major shifts in the structure of each of these segments of the industry over time. This chapter highlights these changes, including shifts in Pakistan's policies on cotton and textiles.

Structure of Exports of Cotton Products

The cotton-to-apparel value chain is the major source of foreign exchange for Pakistan. Over the period 1990–2005, export receipts from these items accounted for an average of more than 60 percent of the country's exports overall (Table 3.1). Output at each step of the value chain is exportable. But there are significant changes in the structure of exports of these items over time. Exports of raw cotton (which includes cotton waste) as a percentage of total export receipts for all cotton products declined from 13.1 percent in 1990–92 to 3.3 percent in 2003–05. The average share of manufactured cotton increased from 86.9 percent to 96.7 percent over the same period.

Within manufactured cotton, major shifts are taking place. Exports of cotton yarn as a share of total exports of cotton-based commodities declined from an average of 29.7 percent in 1990–92 to 13.5 percent in 2003–05. The share of cotton cloth and cotton fabric is above 20 percent. But the share of bedwear exports increased from 6.7 percent in 1990–92 to 17.5 percent in 2003–05. Over the same period, the export share of hosiery increased from 9.5 percent to 19.1 percent. There were also noticeable improvements in the export share of towels and other made-ups. These shifts in the structure of exports indicate that value addition is taking place within the cotton processing industry. This presents an encouraging trend. However, while these developments may be positive, the entire industry faces a set of major challenges.

Performance of Cotton Production

The average annual growth of cotton production in Pakistan between 1990/91 and 2004/05 was 1.4 percent (Table 3.2). A large part of the growth comes from the increase in land area (0.8 percent). The increase in yield is only 0.6 percent, in contrast to more rapid yield growth

Table 3.1 Share of cotton product exports in total Pakistan exports, selected years, 1990–2005

	Average 1990–1992	Average 1995–1997	Average 2003–2005
Exports of all cotton products / total Pakistan exports	61.1	62.6	60.9
Exports of cotton lint / exports of all cotton products[a]	13.1	5.8	3.3
Exports of cotton manufactures / exports of all cotton products	86.9	94.2	96.7
Cotton yarn	29.7	27.7	13.5
Cotton cloth	18.7	23.8	22.0
Tents and canvas	1.7	0.7	0.9
Cotton bags	0.7	0.5	—
Towels	3.3	3.5	5.7
Bedwear	6.7	8.3	17.5
Other made-ups	2.8	3.7	5.2
Apparel, clothing, and garments	13.9	13.0	12.8
Hosiery	9.5	13.1	19.1

Source: Textile Commissioner's Organisation.
[a]Note that values for this row and the next add up to 100 percent.

during the 1970s and 1980s. The overall low growth performance of cotton production is mainly due to poor production performance in Punjab province, where 80 percent of cotton is produced. Production in the province expanded marginally, by only 0.1 percent over the period. The growth of land area devoted to cotton production in Punjab was 0.5 percent. Thus the low growth rate for production in Punjab can be largely attributed to the 0.4 percent decline in yield.

There was a significant drop in production in Punjab in 1993/94 because of an outbreak of the cotton leaf curl virus, which devastated cotton production. The government instituted various preventive and curative measures, but production is nevertheless susceptible to such severe pest infestations. The erratic and low cotton production in the 1990s in the province was largely due to this outbreak, and also to unfavorable weather conditions during the period. The production performance of Sindh province (which produces 20 percent of Pakistan's cotton) is relatively better. The average production growth of 6.8 percent in Sindh over the period was due mainly to an improvement in yield, which rose by an average of 5.4 percent. The expansion in land area devoted to cotton was only 1.4 percent. Compared to Punjab, Sindh was not as seriously affected by pest infestations.

Based on these developments, Salam (2008) argues that one of the major challenges facing Pakistan in cotton production is controlling cotton viruses and other pests. While he acknowledges that there are no simple solutions to the problem, he proposes an integrated approach that includes (1) cultivation of varieties approved for various zones, (2) following recommended planting schedules, (3) uprooting the plants after the final harvest, (4) crop rotation, and (5) judicious use of chemicals. Another potentially important factor could be the adoption of such technological innovations as new, insect-tolerant cotton varieties—in particular Bt cotton. Pakistan has lagged behind other major cotton-producing countries in adopting this recently developed technology.

Table 3.2 Area, production, and yield of cotton in Pakistan, 1990–2005

	All Pakistan			Punjab			Sindh		
Years	Area (thousand ha)	Production (thousand bales)	Yield (kg/ha)	Area (thousand ha)	Production (thousand bales)	Yield (kg/ha)	Area (thousand ha)	Production (thousand bales)	Yield (kg/ha)
1990/91	2,662	9,628	615	2,125	8,501	680	537	1,125	356
1991/92	2,836	12,822	769	2,287	11,417	849	548	1,403	435
1992/93	2,836	9,054	543	2,438	8,237	574	397	816	349
1993/94	2,805	8,041	487	2,249	6,523	493	555	1,517	465
1994/95	2,653	8,697	557	2,244	7,410	561	406	1,282	537
1995/96	2,997	10,595	601	2,463	8,720	602	529	1,862	598
1996/97	3,149	9,374	506	2,540	7,103	475	601	2,250	636
1997/98	2,960	9,184	527	2,348	6,817	494	600	2,336	662
1998/99	2,923	9,790	569	2,283	6,628	494	630	2,134	576
1999/2000	2,983	11,240	641	2,329	8,804	643	634	2,377	637
2000/01	2,928	10,732	623	2,386	8,540	608	524	2,141	695
2001/02	3,116	10,613	579	2,526	8,046	541	547	2,443	759
2002/03	2,794	10,211	621	2,208	7,664	590	543	2,412	755
2003/04	2,991	10,048	571	2,387	7,702	549	561	2,243	680
2004/05	3,229	14,600	769	2,518	11,149	753	635	3,017	808
Mean	2,924	10,309	599	2,355	8,217	594	550	1,957	597
Standard deviation	166	1,652	82	125	1,451	104	71	602	143
Coefficient of variation (%)	5.7	16.0	13.7	5.3	17.7	17.5	13.0	30.8	24.0
Trend growth (%)	0.8	1.4	0.6	0.5	0.1	–0.4	1.4	6.8	5.4
t-statistic	2.9	1.7	0.8	1.6	0.1	–0.3	1.8	5.8	7.8
Minimum	2,653	8,041	487	2,125	6,523	475	397	816	349
Maximum	3,229	14,600	769	2,540	11,417	849	635	3,017	808

Source: Government of Pakistan (2006b).
Note: Growth rates calculated using $\ln Y = a + bt$, where Y is the variable and t is the year.

The economic losses from pest infestations are substantial, especially for the numerous small and marginal cotton farmers. Table 3.3 shows that the average area sown to cotton per farm is 4.9 acres (2 hectares). Farmers operating fewer than 5 acres devote 1.8 acres on average to cotton production. These farms account for 48 percent of the total cotton-growing farms in the country and 18 percent of the total area planted in cotton.

The prices of cotton vary depending on its character, staple, and grade. Character is dependent on the diameter, strength, body, and smoothness of the fibers, as well as maturity (the ratio of mature fibers to immature ones). Staple refers to the fiber length while grade refers to color, brightness, and the amount of foreign matter. Table 3.4 shows the shift in the quality of cotton produced in Pakistan over time, from primarily medium to medium long staple.

Table 3.3 Distribution of cotton-growing farms and cotton area by farm size in Pakistan, 2000

Farm size	Cotton-growing farms as percentage of total farms	Share of total cotton farms (%)	Average area under cotton (acres)	Share of total cotton area (%)
Total private farms (6.62 million)	25	100	4.9	100
Farms up to 5 acres	21	48	1.8	18
Farms of 5–7.5 acres	28	17	3.9	13
Farms of 7.5–12.5 acres	29	16	5.7	19
Farms of 12.5–25 acres	33	12	8.7	21
Farms of 25–50 acres	29	5	15.6	15
Farms of 50 acres and above	25	2	40.2	14

Source: Government of Pakistan (2000).

Table 3.4 Production of cotton by staple length in Pakistan, selected years, 1947–2002 (percent distribution)

Period average	Short: 20.64 mm	Medium: 20.64–25.40 mm	Medium long: 26.19–27.78 mm	Long: 28.57–33.34 mm	Total
1947–70	13.6	82.5	7.4	0.4	100
1970–80	6.2	77.5	15.3	1.0	100
1980–90	2.7	26.4	55.4	15.5	100
1990–92	1.0	6.5	60.3	32.2	100
1995–97	1.0	45.3	52.1	1.5	100
2000–02	0.2	20.4	75.6	3.7	100

Source: Pakistan Central Cotton Committee.

Marketing and Trade Policy

Other factors have affected cotton prices in Pakistan.[1] Foremost of these is government intervention in the price, trade, and marketing system. In 1974 the government established the Cotton Export Corporation (CEC) to control cotton exports. CEC controls prevented the private sector from participating in the international cotton trade until 1986–87, when the role of the CEC diminished while the private sector reemerged. Since 1988–89 the private sector has been able to buy cotton directly from ginners and to both export cotton and sell it domestically.

Prior to 1994 exports of cotton were taxed. The price system on which the export tax was based involved a minimum export price (MEP) and a benchmark price determining the upper price ceiling. The MEP was fixed daily by the Inter-Agency Committee and announced by the State Bank of

[1]This section draws on a more complete analysis of the issues for Pakistan (Cororaton et al. 2008) and a similar assessment for India (Bedi and Cororaton 2008).

Table 3.5 Domestic Pakistan and international nominal and real prices of seed cotton, 1990–2005

	Nominal price (Rs/40 kg)					Real price (Rs/40 kg)			
Years	Support price	Market	Export parity	Import parity	Consumer price index	Support price	Market	Export parity	Import parity
1990/91	245	327	473	592	43.2	567	758	1,096	1,370
1991/92	280	334	408	503	47.4	591	704	861	1,061
1992/93	300	384	385	495	52.1	576	737	739	951
1993/94	315	497	527	772	57.9	544	858	910	1,332
1994/95	400	785	711	1,045	65.5	611	1,198	1,086	1,596
1995/96	400	754	875	995	72.6	551	1,039	1,206	1,371
1996/97	500	793	877	1,085	81.1	616	978	1,082	1,338
1997/98	500	843	838	1,069	87.5	572	964	959	1,222
1998/99	—	914	782	1,030	92.5	—	989	846	1,114
1999/2000	—	641	599	989	95.8	—	669	625	1,033
2000/01	725	900	981	1,184	100.0	725	900	981	1,184
2001/02	780	761	633	971	103.5	753	735	611	938
2002/03	800	914	816	1,239	106.8	749	857	764	1,161
2003/04	850	1,219	1,198	1,477	111.6	761	1,092	1,073	1,323
2004/05	925	885	886	1,180	122.0	758	725	726	967
Mean	540	730	733	975	83	644	880	904	1,197
Standard deviation	243	251	228	277	25	89	160	185	191
Coefficient of variation (%)	45.0	34.4	31.1	28.5	30.2	13.9	18.1	20.4	15.9
Trend growth (%)	—	7.5	5.5	6.1	7.2	—	0.3	−1.7	−1.1
t-statistic	—	5.5	4.0	5.4	16.5	—	0.2	−1.4	−1.2

Sources: Market prices are an average of the prices in important producer area markets during the cotton harvest season, and they are taken from various reports of the Agricultural Prices Commission and the Pakistan Central Cotton Committee. Support prices are adapted from policy reports of the Agricultural Prices Commission and the *Pakistan Journal of Agricultural Economics*. No support price for seed cotton was fixed for the 1998/99 and 1999/2000 crops, while that for the 2000/01 crop was announced by the federal Ministry of Commerce in its Cotton Policy. The consumer price index is taken from the 2004–05 Pakistan Economic Survey and adjusted in light of the 9.28 percent inflation reported for 2004–05 in *Dawn* (August 16, 2005). Real prices are expressed in terms of 2000–01 rupees. The export parity price is the harvest season average, and the import parity price is the annual average, based on international prices of Index B cottons published in the *Cotton Outlook* (various issues). See Orden et al. (2008) for discussions of the export and import parity price calculations.

Pakistan. It was based on international lint prices, domestic yarn and lint prices, the requirements of domestic industry, and the global and local supply situation (Salam 2008). The benchmark price was the ex gin price of lint plus export incidentals. The difference between the MEP and the benchmark price was the basis for the export tax.

This complicated price system was designed to ensure a definite stream of export duty and prevent underinvoicing. It failed in these objectives but suppressed domestic cotton prices relative to international prices by as much as a third (Altaf 2008). Table 3.5 still shows an export parity price higher than the market price in 1990/91 and 1991/92. The pricing system resulted in a transfer of resources from cotton farmers, who received relatively low prices for their raw cotton, to the cotton processing sector, which benefited from relatively low costs for its basic raw material. The price

Figure 3.1 Market, export, and support prices of cotton

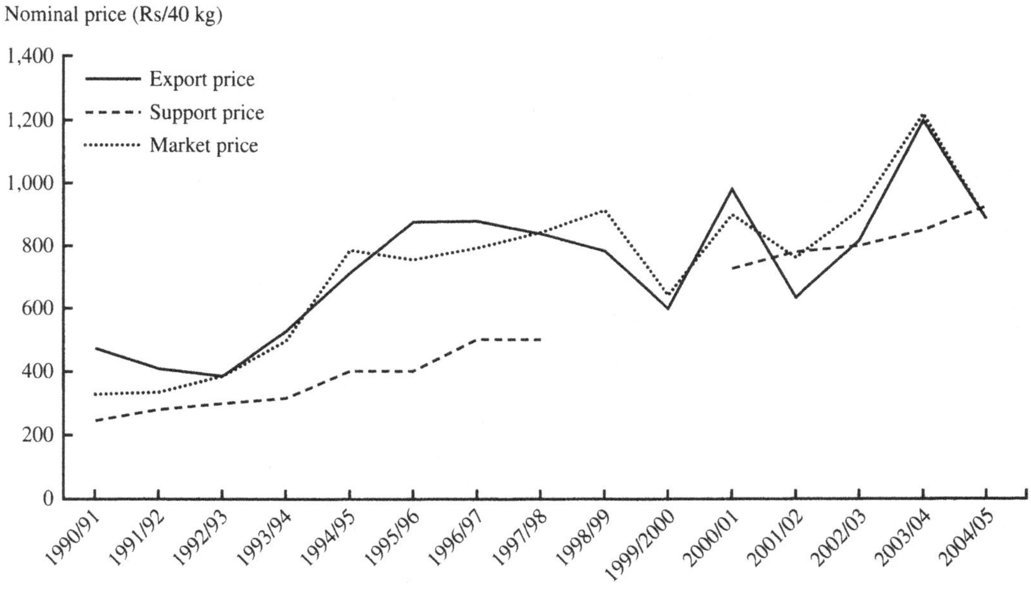

Source: Table 3.5.

intervention system therefore failed to give incentives to the cotton growers.

With the abolition of the export duty on cotton in 1994, domestic prices in the 1994/95 cotton season came closer into line with international prices. In some years since 1994, domestic prices have averaged higher than export prices. At present exports and imports of cotton within the private sector are practically duty free. Government intervention is now limited to the annual review of the support price of seed cotton and limited public-sector procurements to maintain the price, with the intent of at least partially safeguarding the interests of farmers against falling prices.

Figure 3.1 compares the market, export, and support prices of seed cotton. Except for two years (2001/02 and 2004/05), market prices are much higher than support prices. No support prices were fixed in 1998/99, and when the export and market prices fell in 1999/2000 no support price was in effect. Altaf (2008) and Salam (2008) conclude that the benefit of the support price system seems to be more psychological than monetary.

The Ginning Sector

One of the first stages in cotton processing is ginning. In Pakistan most of the early ginners were traders, and their operations were never recognized as a processing industry. At present the ginning sector uses old machinery and primitive saw gins that are maintained by local mechanics. The ginning units are frequently overused and are not replaced in a timely manner, resulting in low-quality cotton lint. Productivity in the ginning sector is low (Altaf 2008): while the international standard for productivity has reached 60 bales per hour, Pakistan is only operating at 10–12 bales per hour. At present 1,221 ginning units are installed; of these, no more than 800 are actually working.

Low cotton quality is also the result of contamination that occurs at various stages of the production and marketing chain. Contaminants in cotton include human and animal hair, bird feathers, cotton twigs, unopened bolls, and leaves. Cotton is contaminated during transportation in open trolleys and trucks, and in the open storage facilities of the ginneries. As a consequence, Pakistan cotton is rated as one of the most contami-

Table 3.6 Installed and working capacity and capacity utilization in the spinning sector, all Pakistan

		Installed capacity (thousands)		Working capacity (thousands)		Capacity utilization (%)	
Years	Units	Spindles	Rotors	Spindles	Rotors	Spindles	Rotors
1958/59	70	1,581	0	1,488	0	—	—
1979/80	187	3,781	16	2,701	14	0.90[a]	0.59
1989/90	266	5,271	72	4,489	64	0.74[b]	0.83
1990/91	277	5,568	75	4,827	67	0.87	0.89
1995/96	503	8,717	143	6,548	80	0.73	0.56
2003/04	456	9,592	146	8,009	66	0.83	0.47
2004/05	458	10,485	155	8,492	79	0.83	0.45

Source: Textile Commissioner's Organisation.
[a]Average capacity utilization for period 1958–79 (spindles and rotors).
[b]Average capacity utilization for period 1980–90 (spindles and rotors).

nated cottons in the world, negatively affecting its price in the international market.

The low quality of cotton lint also results from mixing various cotton varieties procured from farmers. During picking of cotton (it is mostly handpicked by women and children) and storage, the different varieties are seldom kept separate. When traders purchase cotton from farmers in small lots, they seldom transport it separately based on variations in grade or standard. Mixing various lots during marketing reduces quality.

The outdated technology in the ginning sector must be updated. The efficiency of farm management and trading operations must also be increased. To reduce contamination and to improve cotton quality, standardization in cotton processing must be introduced and maintained. That this approach can be beneficial is indicated in the favorable results of a recent project on ginneries in several districts, in which the procedures prescribed by the Pakistan Cotton Standards Institute were followed closely. Salam (2008) has reported that cotton contamination was reduced from 1.94 to 0.74 grams per bale. In 2002 the Cotton Standardization Ordinance was passed. However, it has generally failed to generate favorable results because the textile industry has refused to pay a premium for cotton of higher quality, which in turn has held back progress in the ginning sector.

The Spinning Sector

The cotton lint produced by the ginneries goes to the spinners of yarn. In Pakistan the spinning industry has grown from 70 units in 1958/59 to 458 units in 2004/05 (Table 3.6). Over the same period the number of installed spindles increased from 1.5 million to 10.5 million and the number of installed rotors rose from 0 to 155,000. The capacity utilization of spindles is about 80 percent. The capacity utilization of rotors is much lower.

The increase in capacity in the spinning sector has resulted in significant growth in the production of yarn. Table 3.7 shows that yarn production increased from 376,000 tons in 1972/73 to 2.1 million tons in 2004/05. Furthermore the produced yarn is increasingly used domestically for further processing. The share of yarn going to the export market declined from 49 percent

Table 3.7 Production of and market for Pakistan yarn, selected years, 1972–2005

Years	Production (thousand tons)	Market share (%)		
		Domestic	Exports	Total
1972/73	376	51	49	100
1980/81	375	75	25	100
1990/91	1,055	53	47	100
1995/96	1,475	64	36	100
2003/04	1,939	73	27	100
2004/05	2,087	77	23	100

Source: Textile Commissioner's Organisation.

Table 3.8 Production of yarn (percent distribution)

Period average	Cotton	Cotton waste	Blended		Total
			Polyester/ viscose	Polyester/ cotton	
1972–80	95.2	0.6	0.0	4.2	100
1980–90	88.2	2.1	3.7	6.1	100
1990–92	83.8	1.5	4.9	9.8	100
1995–97	80.7	1.6	6.8	10.9	100
2003–05	75.4	1.3	4.5	18.8	100

Source: Textile Commissioner's Organisation.

in 1972/73 to 23 percent in 2004/05, implying increased value addition in cotton processing.

Over time there has been an increasing trend toward the production of blended yarn in Pakistan. In the 1970s more than 95 percent of the yarn produced was made of pure cotton (Table 3.8). In recent years the share of yarn made of pure cotton dropped to 75 percent. Over these years the share of blended yarn (polyester and cotton) increased to 18.8 percent. However, Pakistan remains behind other major textile manufacturers in the level and diversity of blended yarns and fabrics produced.

The spinning industry in Pakistan produces yarn of all counts (Table 3.9).[2] However, production consists mostly of low counts, which are of relatively low value and hence command a lower price. In the 1970s 57.4 percent of cotton yarn produced was coarse count (sum of count 1s–20s): 23.2 percent in count 20s, 16.4 percent in count 10s, 9.1 percent in count 16s, and small percentages for the other counts under coarse. Some yarns within the medium count were produced, mostly in count 21s. After a decline in the 1980s, the share of cotton count 20s increased slightly in the 1990s and to the present. The share of cot-

[2]Cotton count is a number that indicates the mass per unit length or the length per unit mass of yarn.

Table 3.9 Production of cotton yarn by count in Pakistan, selected years (percent distribution)

Period average	Coarse							Medium						Fine			Super fine			Total
	1–9s	10s	12s	14s	16s	18s	20s	21s	24s	28s	30s	32s	34s	36s	40s	47s	48s	60s	80s	
1971–80	2.6	16.4	3.4	2.3	9.1	0.4	23.2	21.7	0.0	4.2	6.9	4.7	0.3	1.3	2.2	0.2	0.2	0.6	0.2	100
1981–90	3.7	11.3	4.2	4.4	7.6	3.1	8.6	22.2	5.2	5.6	7.5	5.2	4.2	1.9	1.6	1.1	0.5	1.5	0.6	100
1990–92	4.7	10.7	1.6	2.9	9.5	0.7	17.3	22.6	8.1	5.7	9.6	2.6	0.3	1.7	0.8	0.1	0.2	0.9	0.1	100
1995–97	4.6	9.3	2.3	2.4	10.6	2.1	25.7	9.6	6.3	2.6	12.5	4.2	0.8	2.5	2.2	0.2	0.4	0.6	0.9	100
2003–05	7.3	9.2	4.7	2.5	10.7	3.7	25.6	4.9	4.5	3.5	11.0	3.8	1.2	1.0	3.3	0.9	0.6	0.7	1.1	100

Source: Textile Commissioner's Organisation.

Figure 3.2 Average export price of yarn

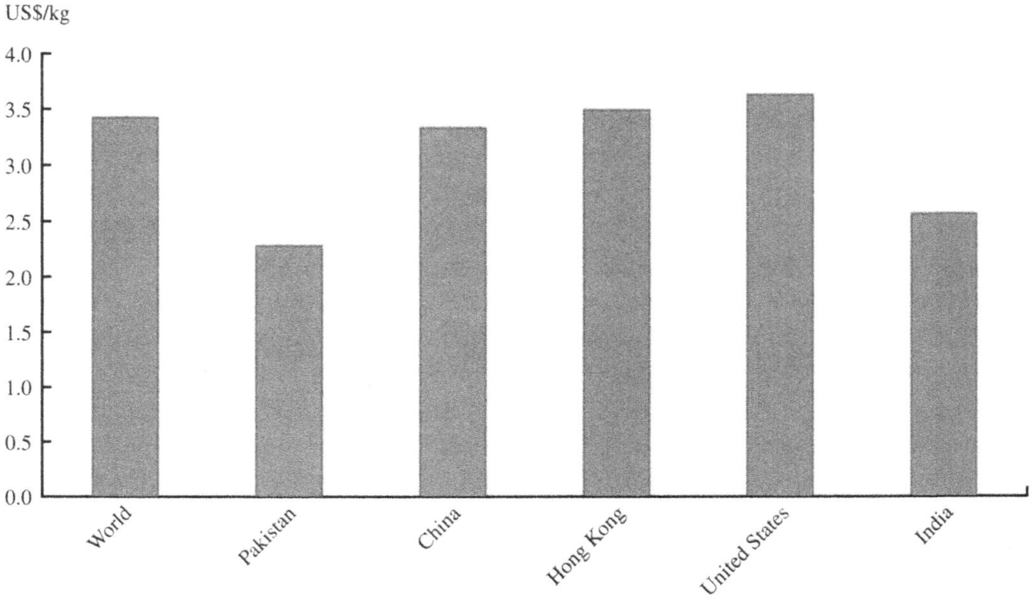

Source: United Nations Comtrade Database.

ton count 30s also improved slightly over the period. However, the share of cotton count 21s and 10s declined.

Figure 3.2 compares the average world export unit price among a few major yarn-producing countries, including Pakistan, between 1990 and 2006. The average price of yarn is US$3.4/kg. The average price for Pakistan yarn (US$2.3/kg) is below the world average. It is also below the average export unit price of the rest of the yarn-exporting countries included in the figure. Altaf (2008) finds a positive return on investment for production of higher-quality yarn. He argues that Pakistani entrepreneurs are not moving sufficiently aggressively into higher-quality production despite the profitability of higher-count yarns. He attributes this outcome to a lack of willingness to take risks, resulting from the historical origins of the industry by government fiat, its subsequent support by the government, and its past reliance on captive markets through the MFA, its preferential access as a supplier to East Pakistan (Bangladesh) before that region gained independence, and protection of the domestic Pakistan market from import competition.

The Fabric/Cloth and Apparel Sectors

The weaving sector in Pakistan is dominated by power looms. Integrated mills, which have their own spinning and dyeing facilities, account for only about 10 percent of total fabric and cloth production.

Over time there has been significant growth in the weaving industry. Production of cloth has increased from 1.191 billion square meters in 1972/73 to 6.833 billion square meters in 2003/04, declining slightly to 6.481 billion square meters in 2004/05 (Table 3.10). About two-thirds of production goes to the domestic market. Preliminary estimates for 2004/05 indicate a higher export share of 42.5 percent.

Pakistan has only a small share of the rapidly growing world market for clothing (Table 3.11). One reason is that production remains concentrated on gray fabric and cloth (Table 3.12). This is unprocessed cloth

Table 3.10 Production of and market for Pakistan cloth, selected years, 1972–2005

Years	Production (billion square meters)	Market (% share)		
		Domestic	Export	Total
1972/73	1.191	69.6[a]	30.4	100
1980/81	1.834	66.8[b]	33.2	100
1990/91	2.854	63.0	37.0	100
1995/96	3.706	64.3	35.7	100
2003/04	6.833	64.7	35.3	100
2004/05	6.481	57.5	42.5	100

Source: Textile Commissioner's Organisation.
[a]Average for period 1972–80.
[b]Average for period 1980–90.

Table 3.11 World exports of clothing, 1996–2004

	1996	1997	1998	1999	2000	2001	2002	2003	2004
World exports (billion US$)	162.6	181.3	180.8	180.3	193.9	196.7	190.8	217.4	233.8
	Share of world exports (%)								
China	15.4	17.5	16.6	16.7	18.6	18.6	21.6	24.0	26.5
India	2.6	2.4	2.6	2.9	3.2	2.8	3.2	3.0	2.8
Bangladesh	1.4	1.5	2.1	n.a.	2.1	2.2	2.1	2.1	1.9
Pakistan	1.2	1.0	1.0	1.0	1.1	1.1	1.2	1.3	1.3

Source: World Trade Organization (2007).
Note: n.a. means not available.

Table 3.12 Production of types of cloth in Pakistan (percent distribution)

Period average	Blended	Gray	Bleached	Dyed and printed	Total
1972–80	1.5	66.3	15.8	16.5	100
1980–90	14.7	55.1	11.2	18.9	100
1990–92	20.6	53.3	5.8	20.4	100
1995–97	17.9	58.4	3.8	19.8	100
2003–05	10.2	51.3	7.7	30.9	100

Source: Textile Commissioner's Organisation.

Table 3.13 Major exporters of bedwear, 1995–2005

	1995	1996	1997	1998	1999	2000	2001	2002	2003	2004	2005
World exports (million US$)	2,754	2,821	3,028	3,153	3,260	3,600	3,752	4,062	4,971	5,401	6,821
						Share of world exports (%)					
China	23.9	21.2	23.4	19.1	21.3	21.8	21.8	20.3	19.9	21.0	27.1
Pakistan	13.7	16.6	16.1	18.0	20.9	20.7	22.2	25.7	27.8	23.8	28.2
Portugal	11.7	11.5	11.7	12.2	11.7	10.3	9.6	8.5	7.3	7.1	5.0
Turkey	4.2	4.6	5.7	6.7	6.6	6.5	6.7	7.1	8.2	9.2	8.1
United States	3.7	3.8	4.0	4.6	3.4	2.8	1.5	2.0	1.7	1.7	1.5
France	3.9	3.7	3.6	3.9	3.9	3.4	2.8	2.6	2.8	2.8	2.2
Mexico	3.1	4.1	4.0	4.2	2.4	1.9	1.4	1.5	1.1	1.2	1.1

Source: World Trade Organization (2007).

that must undergo additional processing to become usable in the production cycle. Although the shares of blended, dyed, and printed cloth have increased, over 50 percent of total fabric and cloth production is still of the gray type. Altaf (2008) argues that the weaving industry remains concentrated on the production of unprocessed fabrics again to avoid risks, in this case the marketing risks associated with more specialized markets, and because of lack of management and marketing expertise. He concludes that the textile sector's "focus on unprocessed products also reflects the gap in their marketing abilities to go into more specialized products. The marketing wing of the weaving mills is very rudimentary. Any change in the amount of greige [gray] cloth means that the marketing of the product must become a specialized aspect of the organization" (Altaf 2008, 77).

Textile Made-ups

One of the textile products that has shown rapid growth for Pakistan in the export market is bedwear. At present this global market is about $7 billion (Table 3.13). In 1995 24 percent of the world market was captured by China; the market share of Pakistan then was almost 14 percent. Pakistan has improved its share of the world market, surpassing China's share as of 2001. By 2005 Pakistan's share was 28.2 percent, while China's was 27.1 percent.

The world market for other textile made-ups is also growing rapidly, from $17 billion in 2001 to $30 billion in 2005 (Table 3.14). This market is dominated by China (34 percent share in 2005), with Pakistan's market share having grown slightly over time to 10 percent. One of the most important items in the category of textile made-ups other than bedwear is towels and cleaning cloths, the world market for which is about $4 billion. While this market is also dominated by China, Pakistan's market share is growing here as well (Table 3.15).

In summary, the cotton-textile industry in Pakistan faces several major challenges. The raw cotton sector is highly susceptible to pest infestation and changes in weather conditions. The cotton lint produced by the ginning sector is of low quality because of outdated technology and contamination. There is an urgent need to update ginning technology and to implement cotton standardization. The yarn produced by the spinning sector is of low count, commanding a low price in the international market.

Table 3.14 Exports of other textile made-ups, 2001–05

	2001	2002	2003	2004	2005
World exports (billion US$)	17.4	19.1	23.5	26.4	30.2
			Share of world exports (%)		
China	21.2	22.9	26.2	29.3	33.9
Pakistan	8.6	9.2	10.0	8.9	10.1
India	6.3	6.6	6.8	6.8	7.9
Turkey	6.0	6.5	6.9	7.0	6.5
Portugal	4.5	4.1	3.5	3.2	2.5

Source: World Trade Organization (2007).

Table 3.15 Major exporters of towels and cleaning cloths, 2002–06

	2002	2003	2004	2005	2006
World exports (million US$)	3,469	3,752	5,025	4,196	3,838
			Share of world exports (%)		
China	23.0	23.1	37.8	23.6	23.8
Pakistan	7.1	8.6	6.1	8.2	9.8
Portugal	9.1	8.0	5.7	6.8	6.9
Turkey	4.3	4.6	5.0	6.5	6.5
Belgium	6.2	5.8	4.7	6.5	6.5
Germany	8.2	7.4	5.2	6.5	5.5
Brazil	4.6	4.5	3.6	3.7	4.1

Source: World Trade Organization (2007).

There are institutional problems in this sector because yarn producers have for so long received substantial support from the government and have operated in protected markets. This support created disincentives to move up to higher counts with higher value in the market. The weaving sector is still producing primarily unprocessed, gray fabric that also commands a relatively low price in the international market. The focus on low-count yarn and unprocessed fabric products reflects risk aversion and a gap in the marketing abilities of firms, preventing them from offering more specialized products. However, there has been good performance in textile made-ups such as bedwear, towels and cleaning cloths, and hosiery.

CHAPTER 4

Poverty in Pakistan

With its relative importance in the economy, the cotton-to-apparel sector will have an important effect on poverty levels in Pakistan. Figure 4.1 shows the recent pattern of poverty incidence. The overall poverty rate declined from 29.1 percent in 1986/87 to 26.1 percent in 1990/91. During these years both urban and rural poverty declined. However, the incidence of rural and urban poverty started to move in different directions in 1993/94. Urban poverty continued to decline, while rural poverty began to rise, widening the gap. The gap reached its peak in 2001/02, largely as a result of a crippling drought in 2000/01, which severely affected agricultural output, together with relatively low international prices for agricultural commodities. In this particular year overall agricultural output shrank. Since almost 70 percent of the people live in rural areas and the majority of them (40 percent of all households nationally) depend on agriculture for income, the incidence of rural poverty increased to 39.1 percent in 2001/02. Urban poverty was generally stable at 22.8 percent.

There is some disagreement about more recent estimates of poverty incidence. For 2004/05, the estimates of the Planning Commission of Pakistan show overall poverty incidence declining from a peak of 34.4 percent in 2001/02 to 23.9 percent in 2004/05. The World Bank (2007) estimates a smaller decline, to 29.2 percent in 2004/05. The disparity between these estimates is due primarily to the inflation factor used in computing the relevant poverty lines. However, the incidence of both urban and rural poverty declines in the most recent years in both estimates.

Cotton is often called the "silver fiber" for Pakistan. Among farmers, about a quarter produce cotton and almost all of these farmers also produce wheat. Nearly 70 percent of the cotton farmers are landowners, while 30 percent are sharecroppers or have other tenancy arrangements. Cotton production is concentrated in a number of primary cotton-producing districts of Punjab and Sindh.

Orden et al. (2008) provide a detailed analysis of income and poverty among cotton farmers based on the 2000–01 HIES data. Consistent with the higher rural poverty rates, they find that incomes are lower for rural than for urban households, that incomes are about equal among farmers and non-farmers, and that among farmers those producing cotton have incomes slightly below the average. Sharecroppers are a particularly disadvantaged group, with over 65 percent of those producing cotton falling into the lowest 40 percent of the national income distribution. Income from cotton is quite important to the cotton-producing households, accounting for nearly 40 percent of total household income among landowners and nearly 45 percent among sharecroppers (Tables 4.1 and 4.2).

Using a partial equilibrium analysis, Orden et al. (2008) evaluated the effects on poverty among cotton-producing households of cotton prices rising by 10–40 percent from their low levels at the time of the 2001–02 HIES. Assuming that the increase in cotton prices will translate into an increase in net income and that the additional income will be used for

Figure 4.1 Poverty trends in Pakistan

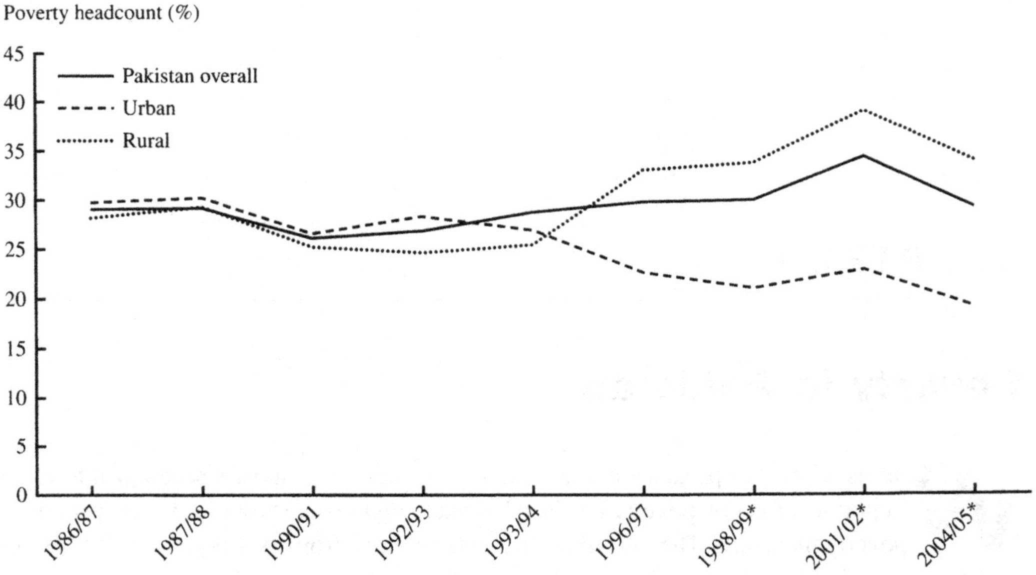

Sources: Government of Pakistan (2003) and World Bank (2007) (*).
Note: Figures for 2004/05 are World Bank estimates.

Table 4.1 Sources of income of landowner cotton-producing households in Pakistan

Sources	National	Punjab All	Punjab Cotton-producing districts[a]	Sindh All	Sindh Cotton-producing districts[b]
Crops	78.9	73.5	75.0	93.7	93.1
Livestock	3.0	6.2	5.4	–5.5	–5.2
Rental	1.4	1.8	1.9	0.3	0.3
Nonfarm business	5.1	6.5	5.1	1.6	1.8
Wages	10.0	9.8	10.0	9.9	10.3
Transfers	1.7	2.2	2.6	0	–0.3
Total (%)	100.0	100	100	100	100
Total (Rs)	77,421	69,672	67,383	108,915	112,575
Crops					
Cotton	48.9	44.4	45.8	56.9	57.3
Wheat	29.5	32.6	32.6	23.9	24
Sugarcane	8.8	6.1	5	14.3	14.1
Rice	1	1.3	1	0.5	0.4
Maize	0.1	0.2	0.2	0	0
Pulses	0.3	0.5	0.4	0	0
Fruits and vegetables	2.1	2.4	2.3	1.5	1.5
Fodder	5.4	7.4	7	1.5	1.3
Other	3.9	5.2	5.2	1.3	1.3
Total	100	100	100	100	100

Source: Orden et al. (2008). Original source of data: 2001–02 Household Integrated Economic Survey.
[a]Bahawalnagar, Bahawalpur, Faisalabad, Jhang, Kasur, D. G. Khan, Khanewal, Layyah, Lodhran Muzaffargrarh, Multan Rajanpur, Okara, Pakpattan, Rahim Yar Khan, Sahiwal, T. T. Singh, and Vehari.
[b]N. Feroze, Ghotki, Hyderabad, Khairpur, Mirpur Khas, Nawabshah, Sanghar, Sukkur, Tharparkar, and Ummarkot.

Table 4.2 Sources of income of sharecropper cotton-producing households in Pakistan

		Punjab		Sindh	
Sources	National	All	Cotton-producing districts	All	Cotton-producing districts
Crops	77.5	59.1	58.2	90.0	90.4
Livestock	–3.4	5.0	5.5	–9.2	–9.4
Rental	1.1	2.5	2.5	0.1	0.1
Nonfarm business	7.5	15.4	15.6	2.1	2.2
Wages	15.6	13.5	13.7	17.0	16.7
Transfers	1.7	4.4	4.5	0.0	0.0
Total (%)	100	100	100	100	100
Total (Rs)	47,123	51,642	52,478	44,488	44,627
Crops					
Cotton	57.5	46.9	47.9	62.2	62.7
Wheat	26.6	38.4	38.0	21.4	21.4
Sugarcane	7.6	1.4	1.4	10.4	10.7
Rice	1.0	1.3	1.2	0.8	0.2
Maize	0.0	0.1	0.1	0.0	0.0
Pulses	0.1	0.2	0.2	0.0	0.0
Fruits and vegetables	0.1	0.4	0.4	0.0	0.0
Fodder	3.9	6.5	5.7	2.8	2.8
Other	3.1	4.9	4.9	2.3	2.3
Total	100	100	100	100	100

Source: Orden et al. (2008). Original source of data: 2001–02 Household Integrated Economic Survey.

consumption expenditures, the direct effects are assessed using the recognized national poverty line and the Foster-Greer-Thorbecke (FGT) measures of poverty (Foster, Greer, and Thorbecke 1984). The analysis focuses on the effects of a 20 percent increase in prices, which reflects the extent to which real cotton prices declined in Pakistan during the late 1990s.

At the national level, initially 40 percent of cotton-producing households are determined to be in poverty. With a 20 percent increase in prices, this percentage declines to 28 percent and the depth (poverty gap) and intensity (poverty gap squared) also decline. In Punjab the decrease due to a 20 percent rise in cotton prices is from 36 percent to 27 percent, while in Sindh it is from 50 percent to 32 percent. Among sharecropper cotton-producing households, poverty declines from 57 percent to 42 percent nationally. Based on these results, Orden et al. (2008) conclude that low cotton prices are an explanation to be taken into account in designing antipoverty strategies and are important on a regional basis, but are only one among several explanations for the overall observed increase in rural poverty. More households produce wheat than cotton in Pakistan, but the net incomes of these households are less dependent on wheat production, and wheat prices affect net household income only for that portion of the crop that is sold commercially. In addition, global wheat prices did not decline as much as global cotton prices in the late 1990s. For these reasons, Orden et al. (2008) find that the effects of cotton prices on households producing cotton are sharper than the effects of changes in wheat prices on households producing wheat during this period.

CHAPTER 5

The CGE Model

The previous chapters have provided a detailed overview of the international cotton and textile markets, the important and interrelated domestic cotton-textile industries, and trends in rural and urban poverty within Pakistan. The report now turns to a quantitative analysis of key developments in the international and domestic economies that have affected the cotton, textile, and apparel sectors in Pakistan and will influence their development in coming years. The analysis is based on a CGE model calibrated to a 2001–02 social accounting matrix (SAM). In this framework we examine the effects of the selected economic determinants on macroeconomic indicators, sectoral output and factor demand, output and factor prices, and household income. Furthermore we examine the implications of these developments for poverty through a microsimulation linking the CGE model results to disaggregated data from the 2001–02 HIES of the Federal Bureau of Statistics (2003).

In transitioning to the CGE analysis it is inevitable that some of the rich detail provided in the foregoing description of the international markets and domestic industry will be lost. The existing SAM for Pakistan, and the CGE model we constructed on this basis, are not sufficiently disaggregated to reflect, for example, the differing performance of Pakistan industry among specific textile products, such as those described earlier. A single-country CGE analysis does not provide an explanation for movements in international capital flows or world cotton and textile prices over time—important developments to which these industries have responded. Such an analysis also cannot provide an explanation of either the political forces that drive government policies toward the sector or the specific scientific, institutional, and management innovations and investments that would raise sectoral productivity. Thus the descriptive background provided in Chapters 2–4 is essential to understanding the relevant scenarios that are to be modeled, to specifying the model parameters and constraints, and to translating the model results back into the detailed economic realities of the country.

But there are also critical insights to be gained from the CGE analysis. The preceding descriptions by themselves do not quantify the linkages among the cotton-textile sectors, responses of the sectors to key developments, or the interactions between these closely related and interdependent sectors. Since the cotton-textile sectors are of significant size in Pakistan, it is also important to take into account the direct and indirect effects on the whole economy of shocks that affect these sectors. The CGE model provides a structured framework for this analysis. Thus the descriptive assessment in the preceding chapters and the model analysis in this and later chapters are complementary in achieving an understanding of these sectors within the Pakistan economy.

This chapter is divided into two parts. The first discusses the structure of the Pakistan CGE model. The detailed specification of the model is presented in Appendix A. The second part presents the structure of the economy in terms of sectoral output, value added, factors of

Figure 5.1 Key relationships in the Pakistan CGE model

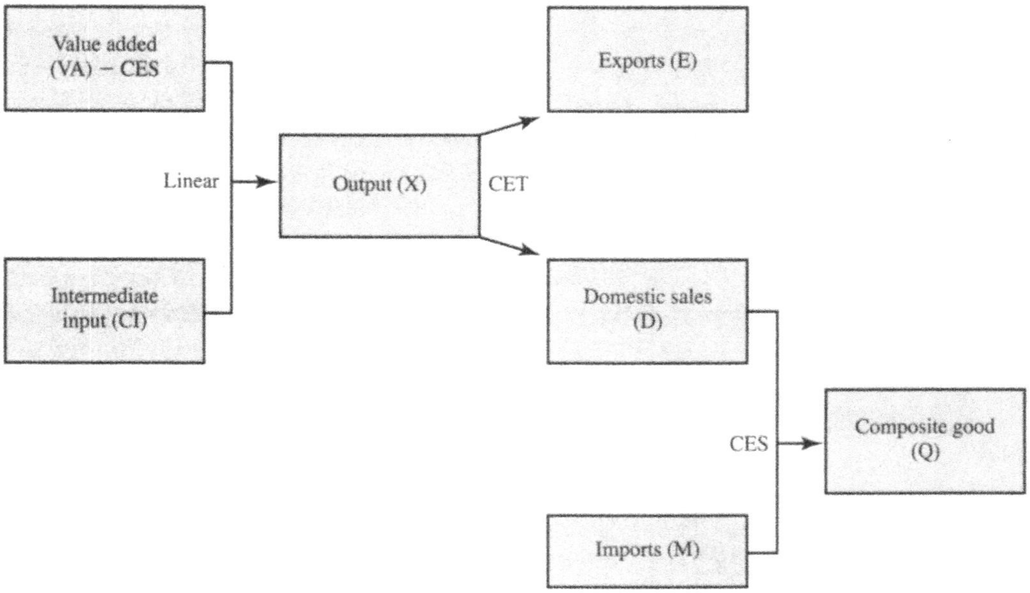

production, foreign trade, and tax structure based on the 2001–02 SAM, along with the key parameters of the model.

Model Specification

The CGE model is calibrated to a 2001–02 SAM constructed by Dorosh, Niazi, and Nazli (2004).[1] The model has 34 production sectors in primary agriculture, lightly processed food, other manufacturing, and services. There are five input categories: three labor types (skilled labor, unskilled workers, and farm labor), capital, and land. There are 19 household categories, a government sector, a firm sector, and the rest of the world.[2]

The basic relationships in the model are shown in Figure 5.1. Output (X) is a composite of value added (VA) and intermediate input (CI). Output is sold to either the domestic market (D) or the export market (E) or both. The model allows for some degree of substitution between E and D through a constant elasticity of transformation (CET) function, with substitution depending on the change in the relative prices of E and D and on the substitution parameter, and a finite elasticity of export demand assumed. Supply in the domestic market comes from two sources: domestic sales (D) and imports (M), with substitution between D and M remaining dependent on the change in the relative prices of D and M and on the substitution parameter through a constant elasticity of substitution (CES) function.

In Figure 5.2 value added in agriculture is a CES function of unskilled labor, capital, and land. Value added in the non-agriculture sector is a CES function of skilled labor, unskilled labor, and capital. In agriculture both capital and land are fixed, while in the non-agriculture sector capital is fixed. Thus in both production functions only the labor input is mobile across sectors.

[1]The specification of the model is generally based on a set of models called EXTER (Decaluwé, Dumont, and Robichaud 2000). There are other CGE specifications, such as the IFPRI Standard CGE Models (Lofgren et al. 2002).

[2]See succeeding tables for detailed listings of production sectors, factor types, and household groups.

Figure 5.2 Output determination in the Pakistan CGE model

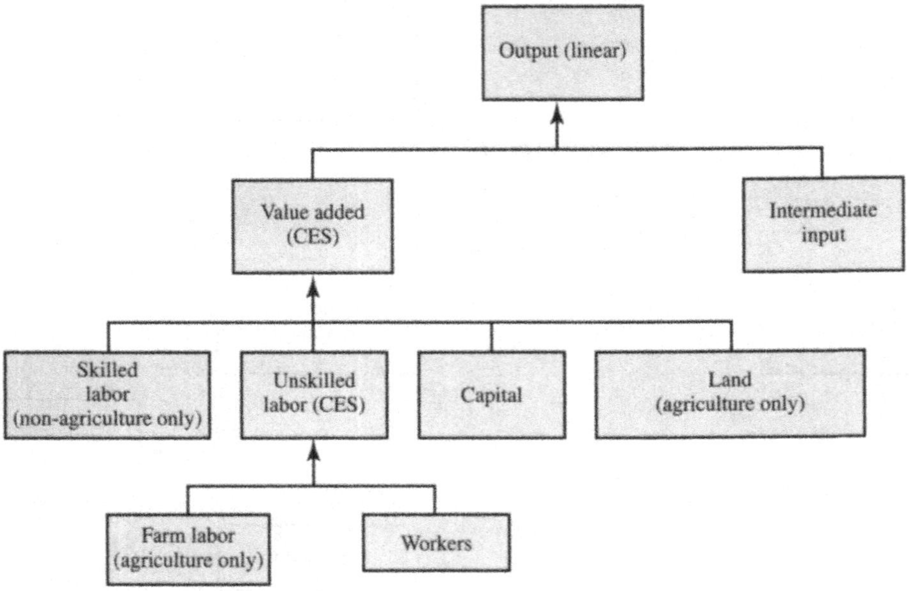

No skilled labor is employed in agriculture, but both skilled and unskilled labor is employed in the non-agriculture sector. Thus skilled labor is mobile across only non-agricultural sectors, while unskilled labor is mobile across all sectors, agriculture and non-agriculture.

Household income sources include factors of production, transfers, foreign remittances, and dividends. Household savings are a fixed proportion of disposable income, and non-poor urban households pay direct income tax to the government. Household demand is represented by the linear expenditure system.

The numeraire is the weighted sectoral value-added price, which we call the Pindex variable. The nominal exchange rate is flexible. Since we assume foreign savings in foreign currency to be fixed, all international transactions are cleared by a real exchange rate variable. Government savings and government total income are both endogenous. However, government consumption in real terms is fixed. Household savings and household income are both endogenous. The income of firms is a portion of total income from capital. We assume savings of firms to be fixed. We further assume dividend payments to domestic households to be endogenous. This implies that changes in the income of firms will translate into changes in dividend payments to domestic households but not to changes in retained earnings of firms.

Economic Structure and Key Parameters in the Model

Table 5.1 shows the sectoral structure of production and trade in the model based on the 2001–02 SAM. There are 12 subsectors in agriculture, 17 in industry, and 5 in the service sector. Given the production structure of the SAM, the cotton-textile industry is captured in the model by three sectors: raw cotton (sector 5), which is classified under agriculture, and cotton lint and yarn (sector 20) and textiles (sector 21), both of which are classified under industry. Drawing on the industry descriptions given earlier, a richer breakdown would separate the ginning of cotton lint from the spinning of cotton yarn as two distinct sectors. The textile sector would distinguish between cotton fabrics and synthetic fabrics because of the rising share of man-made fibers. Furthermore it would be desirable to have a separate apparel sector for apparel, clothing, and garments. This sectoral disaggregation would allow more precise modeling than is feasible at this time of the interactions among the cotton-textile-apparel sectors in the economy.

In terms of overall sectoral value added, total agriculture and industry each have a 23 percent share while the service sector has 53.5 percent. Within agriculture the sector comprising livestock, cattle, and dairy has a 10.3 percent share. Wheat production (irrigated and nonirrigated) has 1.9 percent while raw cotton has 1.4 percent. In industry wheat milling has a 1.2 percent share while the combined share of textile and cotton lint and yarn is 5 percent. Cotton-related sectors therefore have a combined share of 6.4 percent in the overall value added.

Agriculture contributes 20.1 percent to the total value of output. The contribution of industry is 38.4 percent. Within agriculture the combined share of wheat is 1.9 percent; of raw cotton, 1.1 percent; and of livestock, cattle, and dairy, 9.7 percent. Within industry wheat milling has a 4.4 percent share; rice milling (International Rice Research Institute [IRRI] and basmati), 1.2 percent; cotton lint and yarn, 3.3 percent; and textiles, 8.0 percent. The cotton-yarn-apparel sectors therefore have a combined share of 12.4 percent of the overall output.

Agriculture, with 57.4 percent, has a higher value-added ratio than industry, with 30 percent. Among major sectors, service has the highest ratio, 64.3. Within agriculture, forestry and "other major crops" have higher ratios than the rest. Within industry, the ratios are much lower, except for mining, energy, and cement bricks. Industry has generally higher capital-labor ratios than agriculture, except for poultry and livestock, cattle, and dairy. Sectoral employment is also indicated. About 11 percent of labor is employed in agriculture, and 17 percent is employed in industry. Within industry, the major employer is construction (5.5 percent), followed by the textile industry (2.4 percent). Labor is mostly employed in the service sector, with an employment share of 72 percent. Furthermore no skilled labor is employed in agriculture in the SAM. Farm labor accounts for 81 percent of labor in agriculture, except in livestock, poultry, and fishing, where unskilled workers are also employed. The land-output ratio in agriculture varies. The highest land intensity is in forestry, followed by paddy basmati.

Industry has the highest import intensity ratio at 31.4 percent.[3] Within industry, the highest ratio is that for mining at 80.5 percent, because of imports of crude oil. Other manufacturing has 71 percent and chemicals, 69.9 percent. The import intensity ratio of petroleum is also high at 50.1 percent. In terms of import shares, other manufacturing captures 54 percent of the overall imports; chemicals, 11.2 percent; and mining and petroleum refining, about 9 percent each.

How are the cotton-related sectors interrelated and linked with the rest of the economy? Table 5.2 shows the sectoral linkages. The structure of inputs indicates that 61.2 percent of the input requirements of raw cotton are primary inputs (labor, capital, land, and water). Other inputs are from industries other than cotton lint and yarn and textiles. In the case of cotton lint and yarn, 21.6 percent of its input requirements are primary inputs. Thus its value-added component is significantly lower than that for raw cotton. Furthermore the cotton lint and yarn sector buys 30 percent of its input requirements from the raw cotton sector, 23.2 percent from within the sector itself, and 21.6 percent from other sectors that are non-cotton-related. The textile industry does not buy directly from the raw cotton sector. Instead it buys 22.7 percent from the cotton lint and yarn sector, 23.8 percent from within the sector itself, and 31.4 percent from the rest of the industries. From

[3]Import intensity ratio is defined as the sector's imports divided by its total domestic supply.

Table 5.1 Elasticity parameters and production structure

	Production																
												Exports (%)		Imports (%)			
Sectors	Value-added ratio v.a. ÷ x (%)[a]	Value-added share (%)	Output share (%)	Capital-labor ratio[b]	Employmemt share (%)	Share of skilled labor (%)	Share of farmers (%)	Share of workers (%)	Land-output ratio (%)	sig_va[c]	Indirect tax rate (%)	sig_m[d]	sig_e[e]	Share	Intensity[f]	Share	Intensity[g]
1. Wheat, irrigated	50.8	1.8	1.8	0.3	1.6	—	81.1	18.9	27.8	0.75	0.10	0.75	1.25	0.6	3.6	0.3	2.5
2. Wheat, nonirrigated	50.9	0.1	0.1	0.3	0.1	—	81.1	18.9	27.2	0.75	0.00	—	—	—	—	—	—
3. Paddy, IRRI	60.2	0.2	0.2	0.5	0.1	—	81.2	18.8	45.4	0.75	0.30	—	—	—	—	—	—
4. Paddy, basmati	60.2	0.5	0.4	0.5	0.1	—	81.1	18.9	51.3	0.75	0.00	—	—	—	—	—	—
5. Raw cotton	61.2	1.4	1.1	0.3	1.1	—	81.1	18.9	36.0	0.75	0.04	—	—	—	—	—	—
6. Sugarcane	60.0	1.0	0.8	0.7	0.3	—	81.1	18.9	46.7	0.75	0.07	—	—	—	—	—	—
7. Other major crops	71.0	2.8	2.0	0.3	2.4	—	81.1	18.9	38.9	0.75	0.05	0.75	1.25	0.5	2.7	0.6	4.5
8. Fruits and vegetables	64.2	3.6	2.8	0.6	1.8	—	81.1	18.9	44.4	0.75	0.34	0.75	1.25	1.1	3.8	1.3	6.9
9. Livestock, cattle, and dairy	53.2	10.3	9.7	9.0	2.6	—	—	100.0	—	0.75	0.00	0.75	1.25	0.1	0.1	0.7	1.1
10. Poultry	51.6	0.7	0.7	9.0	0.2	—	—	100.0	—	0.75	0.00	0.75	1.25	0.0	0.1	0.0	0.0
11. Forestry	82.1	0.3	0.2	0.0	0.1	—	81.1	18.9	65.7	0.75	0.00	0.75	1.25	0.5	31.4	0.2	25.2
12. Fishing industry	57.1	0.6	0.5	2.3	0.4	—	—	100.0	—	0.75	0.00	0.50	1.25	1.1	23.8	0.0	0.1
Agriculture	57.4	23.2	20.1	—	10.7	—	—	—	—	—	—	—	—	3.9	1.9	3.1	2.4
13. Mining	74.6	0.6	0.4	2.3	0.5	85.0	—	15.0	—	0.75	14.50	0.50	2.00	0.8	18.6	9.3	80.5
14. Vegetable oil	7.9	0.2	1.4	6.7	0.1	60.3	—	39.7	—	1.50	0.02	1.50	2.00	0.0	0.0	2.3	20.0
15. Wheat milling	21.8	1.2	2.8	4.4	0.6	64.9	—	35.1	—	1.50	0.02	1.50	2.00	0.5	1.8	0.8	4.3
16. Rice milling, IRRI	30.7	0.2	0.4	3.7	0.1	56.8	—	43.2	—	1.50	0.00	—	2.00	1.7	46.6	0.0	0.0

17. Rice milling, basmati	29.0	0.5	0.8	3.7	0.3	56.8	—	43.2	—	1.50	0.00	—	2.00	2.3	28.6	0.0	0.0
18. Sugar	32.2	1.4	2.2	3.3	0.8	70.0	—	30.0	—	1.50	6.75	1.50	2.00	0.0	0.1	0.3	1.9
19. Other food	36.9	1.7	2.3	4.7	0.8	61.6	—	38.4	—	1.50	44.69	1.50	2.00	12.1	51.5	1.1	12.4
20. Cotton lint and yarn	21.6	1.4	3.3	3.3	0.8	85.5	—	14.5	—	1.50	12.05	1.50	2.00	9.0	27.1	0.7	4.3
21. Textiles	22.2	3.6	8.0	2.7	2.4	78.9	—	21.1	—	1.50	0.00	1.50	2.00	31.9	39.7	1.6	4.8
22. Leather	8.3	0.1	0.5	2.9	0.1	60.4	—	39.6	—	1.50	0.00	1.50	2.00	2.3	42.8	0.1	5.2
23. Wood products	36.3	0.7	0.9	1.8	0.6	68.0	—	32.0	—	0.50	0.18	1.50	2.00	0.0	0.3	0.6	8.6
24. Chemicals	28.2	0.5	0.9	3.8	0.3	55.2	—	44.8	—	0.50	2.58	0.50	2.00	1.4	15.9	11.2	69.9
25. Cement and bricks	55.0	1.4	1.3	7.4	0.4	69.0	—	31.0	—	0.50	24.15	—	2.00	0.0	0.2	—	—
26. Petroleum refining	19.4	0.6	1.5	2.9	0.4	71.9	—	28.1	—	0.50	28.96	0.50	—	—	—	9.7	50.1
27. Other manufacturing	25.4	2.6	5.0	2.6	1.7	68.0	—	32.0	—	0.50	4.39	0.50	2.00	16.6	33.2	54.0	71.0
28. Energy	60.8	3.4	2.8	4.0	1.7	80.0		20.0	—	0.50	5.02	—	—	—	—	—	—
29. Construction	41.6	3.2	3.8	0.4	5.5	50.0	—	50.0	—	1.50	0.16	—	—	—	—	—	—
Industry	30.3	23.3	38.4	—	16.9	—	—	—	—	—	—	—	—	78.6	20.5	91.6	31.4
30. Commerce	84.0	15.3	9.1	0.4	26.5	20.0	—	80.0	—	0.50	0.00	2.00	0.50	0.1	0.1	0.2	0.4
31. Transportation	53.9	11.8	10.9	1.5	11.7	20.0	—	80.0	—	1.25	0.27	—	0.50	17.4	15.9	—	—
32. Housing	81.8	4.9	3.0	—	—	—	—	—	—	1.25	0.03	—	—	—	—	—	—
33. Private services	53.5	12.9	12.0	1.5	12.8	20.0	—	80.0	—	1.25	0.00	—	—	0.0	0.0	5.0	6.0
34. Public services	66.2	8.6	6.5	—	21.4	100.0	—	—	—	1.25	0.00	1.25	0.50	—	—	—	—
Services	64.3	53.5	41.5	—	72.4	—	—	—	—	—	—	—	—	17.5	4.2	5.2	2.0
Total	49.8	100.0	100.0	—	100.0	—	—	—	—	—	—	—	—	100.0	10.0	100.0	14.5

Source: 2001–02 social accounting matrix of Pakistan.

[a]v.a. is value added; x is output. [b]Total labor ÷ total capital. [c]Substitution parameter in CES value-added function. [d]Substitution parameter in CES composite good function.

[e]Substitution parameter CET. [f]Export ÷ output. [g]Imports ÷ composite good.

Table 5.2 Linkages of cotton-related sectors with the rest of the economy

Structure of input	Raw cotton	Cotton lint and yarn	Textiles
Intermediate input			
Raw cotton	—	30.0	0.0
Lint and yarn	1.6	23.2	22.7
Textiles	—	0.5	23.8
Others	37.1	24.6	31.4
Primary input (value added)	61.2	21.6	22.2
Skilled labor	—	4.3	4.8
Unskilled labor	17.5	0.7	1.3
Farm labor	14.2	—	—
Workers	3.3	0.7	1.3
Capital	5.4	16.6	16.1
Land	27.8	—	—
Total	100.0	100.0	100.0
Household consumption/sector's total domestic demand (%)	—	0.4	54.8
Imports/total supply (%)	—	4.3	4.8
Exports/total output (%)	—	27.1	39.7

Source: 2001–02 social accounting matrix of Pakistan.

these ratios, the indirect link between the textile and raw cotton sectors through cotton lint and yarn is only 6.8 percent (0.30 × 22.7). Its primary input requirement is 22.2 percent. Similar to cotton lint and yarn, its value-added component is relatively smaller than that for raw cotton.

The sectoral indirect tax structure is presented in Table 5.1. The highest tax rate of 44.69 percent is on "other food." From Table 5.3, the share of other food in the consumption of households is only about 1 percent. Indirect taxes are also relatively high on cement and bricks and petroleum refining, which generally account for less than 1 percent of household consumption directly but affect housing and transportation costs. The tax rate on sugar is 6.75 percent, and its share in the consumer basket ranges from 3.3 percent to 9.6 percent among the 19 household types. The tax rate on cotton lint and yarn is 12.05 percent, while the rate on textiles is zero. However, since cotton lint and yarn are major inputs into textile production, an increase in the tax will increase the cost of production of textiles. This will affect consumers since the share of textiles in the consumption basket is about 5 percent.

The other price distortions are tariffs. Vegetable oil has the highest tariff rate of 44.2 percent. Another important commodity that has high tariffs, averaging 27 percent, is "fruits and vegetables." This commodity accounts for a larger share in the consumption basket of households. Other major commodities that have high tariffs and substantial consumption shares are textiles (13.7 percent) and other food items (9.4 percent).

A composite sector of livestock, cattle, and dairy has the highest share in the consumption basket, but it varies across household groups from 14.4 percent in large and medium farm groups h3 and h6 to 24.9

Table 5.3 Consumption share (percent)

Commodities	h1	h2	h3	h4	h5	h6	h7	h8	h9	h10	h11	h12	h13	h14	h15	h16	h17	h18	h19
Other major crops	0.1	0.1	0.1	0.1	0.1	0.1	0.1	0.1	0.2	0.2	0.1	0.2	0.2	0.1	0.3	0.2	0.2	0.2	0.2
Fruits and vegetables	4.8	4.4	5.7	4.8	4.4	5.7	5.6	5.2	6.1	6.6	6.2	7.0	6.0	6.5	7.1	6.0	6.7	6.2	6.9
Livestock, cattle, and dairy	19.9	22.8	14.4	19.9	22.8	14.4	19.5	26.1	21.6	19.3	22.3	17.5	20.7	24.9	15.9	19.9	17.9	18.3	18.0
Poultry	1.1	1.2	1.7	1.1	1.2	1.7	1.1	1.0	1.4	1.0	1.0	1.4	0.7	0.9	1.5	1.4	1.0	1.7	1.1
Forestry	0.0	0.1	0.0	0.0	0.1	0.0	0.0	0.1	0.1	0.0	0.0	0.1	0.0	0.0	0.0	0.1	0.0	0.0	0.0
Fishing industry	1.9	0.0	0.5	1.9	0.0	0.5	2.5	0.0	0.1	2.7	0.0	0.2	1.2	—	0.3	0.9	0.7	0.8	0.6
Mining	0.0	0.0	0.0	0.0	0.0	0.0	0.0	0.0	0.0	0.0	0.0	0.0	0.0	0.0	0.0	0.0	0.0	0.0	0.0
Vegetable oil	2.9	2.8	2.7	2.9	2.8	2.7	3.3	3.3	3.3	3.4	3.6	3.4	3.2	3.4	3.8	3.2	3.9	2.7	3.8
Wheat milling	6.9	4.4	7.5	6.9	4.4	7.5	6.6	6.4	7.4	8.2	7.7	8.3	10.9	9.1	11.7	6.0	10.3	4.0	9.1
Rice milling, IRRI	0.7	0.2	0.2	0.7	0.2	0.2	1.2	0.2	0.2	1.1	0.2	0.2	0.6	0.3	0.1	0.3	0.5	0.2	0.4
Rice milling, basmati	2.5	0.6	0.7	2.5	0.6	0.7	4.2	0.8	0.8	4.0	0.8	0.7	2.3	1.0	0.5	1.1	1.7	0.9	1.5
Sugar	5.0	3.6	5.3	5.0	3.6	5.3	4.9	4.8	7.3	5.9	5.5	8.2	8.2	5.8	9.6	5.0	7.0	3.3	5.8
Other food	1.2	0.9	1.3	1.2	0.9	1.3	1.2	1.0	1.9	1.6	1.2	1.9	1.5	1.0	2.2	1.6	1.5	1.9	1.6
Textiles	5.5	6.6	4.9	5.5	6.6	4.9	6.0	6.2	5.3	6.7	6.5	5.3	6.1	6.8	5.1	5.8	6.6	5.8	6.8
Leather	0.2	0.4	0.3	0.2	0.4	0.3	0.2	0.3	0.3	0.3	0.3	0.3	0.2	0.4	0.3	0.3	0.3	0.3	0.4
Chemicals	3.0	4.3	4.9	3.0	4.3	4.9	1.9	2.2	1.8	0.5	2.1	2.3	0.4	0.9	1.2	2.9	1.3	3.5	1.4
Cement and bricks	0.9	1.2	1.4	0.9	1.2	1.4	0.5	0.6	0.5	0.1	0.6	0.6	0.1	0.3	0.3	0.8	0.4	1.0	0.4
Petroleum refining	0.5	0.5	0.6	0.5	0.5	0.6	0.5	0.6	0.8	0.7	0.7	0.8	0.6	0.6	0.8	0.8	0.8	0.9	1.0
Other manufacturing	5.8	8.4	9.6	5.8	8.4	9.6	3.7	4.4	3.5	1.0	4.0	4.4	0.8	1.8	2.2	5.7	2.5	6.9	2.7
Energy	0.6	0.7	0.7	0.6	0.7	0.7	0.6	0.7	1.0	0.9	0.8	0.9	0.8	0.7	1.0	0.9	1.0	1.1	1.2
Commerce	3.5	3.5	3.5	3.5	3.5	3.5	3.5	3.5	3.5	3.4	3.5	3.5	3.4	3.4	3.4	3.5	3.4	3.4	3.4
Transportation	13.5	13.6	13.6	13.5	13.6	13.6	13.3	13.4	13.3	13.1	13.3	13.3	13.1	13.1	13.2	13.4	13.2	13.1	13.0
Housing	1.4	1.6	2.4	1.4	1.6	2.4	1.5	1.3	1.8	1.9	1.7	1.8	1.6	1.5	1.8	2.5	1.7	6.3	3.5
Private services	14.5	14.7	14.6	14.5	14.7	14.6	14.4	14.4	14.4	14.2	14.4	14.4	14.1	14.2	14.3	14.4	14.3	14.1	14.1
Public services	3.4	3.4	3.4	3.4	3.4	3.4	3.4	3.4	3.4	3.3	3.3	3.4	3.3	3.3	3.3	3.4	3.3	3.3	3.3
Total	100	100	100	100	100	100	100	100	100	100	100	100	100	100	100	100	100	100	100

Source: 2001–02 social accounting matrix of Pakistan.
Notes: See Table 5.4 for definitions of groups h1–h19. IRRI is International Rice Research Institute.

percent in agricultural worker group h14. The other major items in the consumption basket of households are private services (about 14 percent), transportation (about 13 percent), wheat milling (from 4 percent among urban non-poor h18 to 11.7 percent among agricultural workers h15), textiles (from 4.9 percent in h3 and h6 to 6.8 percent among agricultural workers h14 and urban poor h19), other manufacturing (from 0.8 percent among agricultural workers h13 to 9.6 percent among large and medium farmers h3 and h6), sugar (from 3.3 percent in h18 to 9.6 percent among agricultural workers h15), and fruits and vegetables (from 4.4 percent among large and medium farms h2 and h5 to 7.1 percent in h15).

Overall the foreign trade sector is not very large relative to the domestic sector. Of the total domestic output, only 10 percent goes to the export market. Of the total goods and services available in the market, only 14.5 percent is imported. However, there are large differences across sectors. For example, within agriculture, the export intensity ratio of forestry is 31.4 percent and that of fishing, 23.8 percent.[4] The export intensity ranges from 2.7 percent to 3.8 percent among "other major crops," irrigated wheat, and fruits and vegetables, while it is very small for the rest of the sectors. The overall ratio for agriculture is only 1.9 percent. Within industry, "other food" has the highest ratio, at 51.5 percent. Rice milling (IRRI) has a ratio of 46.6 percent; leather, 42.8 percent; textiles, 39.7 percent; and cotton lint and yarn, 27.1 percent. The textile sector dominates exports. In the SAM, textile exports have a 31.9 percent share of the total—dominant but less than that indicated in the WTO data. Cotton lint and yarn has a 9 percent export share, while the share for other food is 12.1 percent.

Table 5.1 also includes values of key elasticity parameters in the model: the production substitution elasticity (sig_va), import substitution elasticity (sig_m), and export transformation elasticity (sig_e). Some of the parameter values were used in Robinson et al. (1997). Annabi, Cockburn, and Decaluwé (2006) provide a survey of parameter values often used in CGE models, on which we also draw. The elasticities in Keeney and Hertel (2004), which are estimated econometrically, are a bit higher. Our model also reflects a careful assessment of parameters adopted for raw cotton (sig_va) and cotton lint and yarn and textiles (sig_va and sig_e) to reflect the close movement of domestic cotton lint prices with international prices (described earlier) since the export policy reforms in the 1990s. This selection of parameters is described in Appendix B.

There are 19 household groups in the model. The agriculture-based groups are categorized by household location (Punjab, Sindh, and other Pakistan) and size of landholdings (large, medium, and small farms; landless small-farm renters; and agricultural workers without land). In addition there are four national aggregates: rural nonfarm poor and non-poor and urban poor and non-poor. Table 5.4 lists the 19 households in the SAM and the corresponding characteristics of these 19 household groups in the HIES.

The sources of household income in the model are labor income, capital income, income from land and water, dividend income, and income from the rest of the world (Table 5.5). There are 10 labor types. The original SAM has four types of capital, but in the model all these are aggregated into one factor. Similarly the original SAM has 12 categories of land, but they are aggregated into one factor in the model.

About three-fourths of the income of the urban poor comes from unskilled labor wages, and about 18 percent from capital, which is essentially informal capital. Major sources of income for urban non-poor households include dividend income

[4]Export intensity ratio is defined as the sector's exports divided by its output.

Table 5.4 Household categories in social accounting matrix and Household Integrated Economic Survey

Categories	2001–02 social accounting matrix	2001–02 Household Integrated Economic Survey
	Large farmers	**Landowners with more than 50 acres**
h1	Sindh[a]	
h2	Punjab	
h3	Other Pakistan	
	Medium farmers	**Landowners with more than 12.5 acres but less than 50 acres**
h4	Sindh	
h5	Punjab	
h6	Other Pakistan	
	Small farmers	**Landowners with more than 0 acres but less than 12.5 acres**
h7	Sindh	
h8	Punjab	
h9	Other Pakistan	
	Small farm renters and landless	**No landholdings, but rented land for farm activities**
h10	Sindh	
h11	Punjab	
h12	Other Pakistan	
	Rural agricultural workers and landless	**No landholdings, agricultural workers**
h13	Sindh	
h14	Punjab	
h15	Other Pakistan	
	Rural non-farmers	
h16	Non-poor	Rural non-poor, non-farmers and nonagricultural workers
h17	Poor	Rural poor, non-farmers and nonagricultural workers
	Urban	
h18	Non-poor	Urban non-poor
h19	Poor	Urban poor

Sources: 2001–02 social accounting matrix and 2001–02 Household Integrated Economic Survey of Pakistan.
[a]The three major provinces are Punjab, Sindh, and other Pakistan, which includes Azad Kashmir, Balochistan, the Northern Areas, the North-West Frontier Province, federally administered areas, and federally administered tribal areas.

Table 5.5 Sources of household income and income tax (percent)

Households	2001–02 income: Total (million Rs)	2001–02 income: Per capita (thousand Rs)	2001–02 population: Number (thousands)	2001–02 population: Percent distribution	Labor categories[a]: L1	L2	L3	L4	L5	L6	L7	L8	L9	L10	Capital	Land	Dividend income	Government transfers	Income from abroad	Direct tax
Large farmers																				
Sindh	19,079	112.9	169	0.12	13.2	—	—	—	—	—	—	0.1	0.2	—	31.4	49.8	—	0.00	5.31	—
Punjab	64,116	173.7	369	0.25	8.6	—	—	—	—	—	—	—	0.5	—	43.3	42.2	—	0.07	5.30	—
Other Pakistan	10,755	152.9	70	0.05	9.8	—	—	—	—	—	—	0.0	0.1	—	52.4	32.3	—	0.10	5.31	—
Medium farmers																				
Sindh	44,625	30.4	1,466	1.00	—	14.5	—	—	—	—	—	0.5	2.6	—	39.6	37.4	—	0.04	5.30	—
Punjab	145,995	48.4	3,014	2.07	—	—	10.8	—	—	—	—	0.0	4.3	—	52.3	27.2	—	0.10	5.30	—
Other Pakistan	35,572	34.2	1,040	0.71	—	—	—	14.9	—	—	—	1.0	1.9	—	38.2	38.4	—	0.23	5.30	—
Small farmers																				
Sindh	57,648	14.9	3,873	2.65	—	—	—	—	6.8	—	—	4.3	4.7	—	57.9	20.4	—	0.54	5.30	—
Punjab	318,888	18.1	17,605	12.06	—	—	—	—	—	7.9	—	4.2	10.0	—	51.8	20.3	—	0.55	5.30	—
Other Pakistan	124,985	11.9	10,493	7.19	—	—	—	—	—	—	6.0	3.4	8.2	—	63.6	12.5	—	0.95	5.30	—

Small farm renters																				
Sindh	43,672	7.7	5,682	3.89	—	—	—	—	11.6	—	—	14.7	4.0	—	48.5	15.6	—	0.36	5.31	—
Punjab	45,963	10.7	4,307	2.95	—	—	—	—	—	9.0	—	6.1	14.3	—	48.7	16.1	—	0.45	5.30	—
Other Pakistan	14,970	8.2	1,818	1.25	—	—	—	—	—	—	10.1	2.3	12.2	—	55.0	14.7	—	0.35	5.32	—
Rural agricultural workers																				
Sindh	20,782	6.4	3,241	2.22	—	—	—	—	—	—	—	36.0	15.1	—	42.8	—	—	0.89	5.30	—
Punjab	68,172	12.0	5,693	3.90	—	—	—	—	—	—	—	33.6	15.7	—	45.2	—	—	0.20	5.30	—
Other Pakistan	9,513	14.6	653	0.45	—	—	—	—	—	—	—	15.6	3.1	—	76.0	—	—	0.06	5.32	—
Rural non-farmers																				
Non-poor	400,771	19.8	20,233	13.86	—	—	—	—	—	—	—	—	43.0	—	49.9	—	—	1.86	5.30	—
Poor	134,398	5.5	24,525	16.80	—	—	—	—	—	—	—	—	29.7	—	63.4	—	—	1.56	5.30	—
Urban																				
Non-poor	1,744,119	58.5	29,829	20.44	—	—	—	—	—	—	—	—	11.9	33.3	10.6	—	38.05	0.84	5.30	8.4
Poor	181,413	15.3	11,880	8.14	—	—	—	—	—	—	—	—	76.2	—	18.0	—	—	0.47	5.30	—

Source: 2001–02 social accounting matrix of Pakistan.

[a]Labor categories: L1, own farm labor, large farm; L2, own farm labor, medium farm, Sindh; L3, own farm labor, medium farm, Punjab; L4, own farm labor, medium farm, other Pakistan; L5, own farm labor, small farm, Sindh; L6, own farm labor, small farm, Punjab; L7, own farm labor, small farm, other Pakistan; L8, labor, primary agricultural wage; L9, labor, unskilled wage; L10, labor, skilled wage.

(38.0 percent) and skilled labor wages (33.3 percent). About 12 percent of their income comes from unskilled labor wages and about 11 percent from (nondividend) capital. Rural nonfarm households, both poor and non-poor, have unskilled labor wages and informal capital as major sources of their income. For the rural nonfarm poor 63.4 percent of their income comes from informal capital, while for the rural nonfarm non-poor this level is only 50 percent.

Rural agricultural workers obtain a major part of their income from primary-agriculture labor wages, informal capital, and to some extent unskilled (non-farm) labor wages. Farm households, including small-farm renters, obtain their income from informal capital, land and water, and own-farm labor to various degrees. Only large farms in Punjab and Sindh earn returns to water, while capital income exceeds land income (and often by a large amount) for all farm household groups but one. Own-farm and wage labor accounts for a relatively small share of the income of farm households. In the 2001–02 SAM, all household groups are assumed to obtain 5.3 percent of their income from foreign sources.[5] The structure of direct taxes on households is also shown in Table 5.5. In the SAM only the urban non-poor are paying direct income tax, at the rate of 8.4 percent.

Table 5.6 Sources of government revenue

Source	Share (%)
Indirect tax revenue	49.3
Import tax revenue	10.8
Direct income tax revenue	32.8
Other revenue (water)	7.2
Total	100.0

Source: 2001–02 social accounting matrix of Pakistan.

In the SAM the sources of government revenue include indirect tax revenue (49.3 percent), import tax revenue (10.8 percent), direct income tax revenue (32.8 percent, from urban non-poor households only), and other revenue (7.2 percent, from water) (Table 5.6). In the model water is considered part of land.

[5]The equal-proportionate distribution of foreign source income is a simplification in the SAM that merits further evaluation in light of the high levels of capital inflows and remittances to Pakistan in recent years.

CHAPTER 6

Microsimulations

There are several approaches to linking CGE models with data in a household survey to analyze poverty issues. One is the top-down method, in which the results of CGE models with representative households are applied recursively to data in the household survey grouped into these representative household categories with no feedback effects. Within the top-down method there are wide variations. An early variant of the method was to assume a lognormal distribution of income within a household category where the variance is estimated from the data in the survey (De Janvry, Sadoulet, and Fargeix 1991).[1]

In this method the change in income of the representative household generated in the CGE model is used to estimate the change in the average income for each household category, while the variance of this income is assumed to be fixed. Decaluwé, Dumont, and Savard (1999) argue that a beta distribution is preferable to other distributions, such as the lognormal, because it can be skewed left or right and thus may better represent the types of intracategory income distributions commonly observed. Annabi et al. (2006); Cockburn et al. (2006); Cororaton, Cockburn, and Corong (2006); and Emini, Cockburn, and Decaluwé (2006), among others, apply a top-down approach that utilizes the actual incomes from a household survey and applies the changes in incomes and consumer prices of the representative households generated in the CGE model to each individual household in that category.

The top-down method usually uses CGE models with a limited number of representative households. One criticism of this approach is that it does not account for the heterogeneity of income sources and consumption patterns of the households within each category. Intracategory income variances could be a significant part of the total income variance. That is, there is evidence that households within a given category, as well as across categories, may be affected quite differently according to their asset profiles, location, composition, education, or other characteristics.

To address this issue an integrated CGE microsimulation allows full integration of all households in the survey into the CGE model equilibrium. As demonstrated by Cockburn (2001) and Cororaton and Cockburn (2007), although the full integration approach adds substantially to the computations in the model, it poses no particular technical difficulties because it involves constructing a standard CGE model with as many household categories as there are households in the household survey providing the base data. The fully integrated approach also has some advantages. Decaluwé, Dumont, and Savard (1999), for example, constructed an integrated CGE microsimulation in which 150 households are directly modeled within a CGE model using fabricated data from an archetypal developing country.

[1]Many papers use various types of CGE microsimulations in poverty analysis. In this section we cite only a few of these papers.

They construct the model to allow comparisons with the earlier approaches of multiple household categories and fixed intracategory income distributions. They find that intracategory variations can be important in this context.

Recent more advanced microsimulation methods link CGE models with household data to analyze poverty issues through a sophisticated treatment of the labor market transmission channel. Ganuza, Barros, and Vos (2002) introduce a randomized process to simulate the effects of changes in the labor market structure. Random numbers are used to determine key parameters in the labor market, such as: (1) which persons of working age change their labor force status, (2) who will change occupational category, (3) which employed persons obtain different levels of education, and (4) how new mean labor incomes are assigned to individuals in the sample. The random process is repeated a number of times in a Monte Carlo fashion to construct 95 percent confidence intervals for the indexes of poverty. The CGE model is used to quantify the effects of a macroeconomic shock on key labor market variables, such as wages and employment, and these results are applied in the microsimulation process.

In this report we follow the straightforward top-down approach, in which the changes in incomes from various sources and consumer prices of the representative households, as generated in the CGE model, are applied to the actual distribution in the household survey. Thus, recursively, we introduce the CGE results on household incomes and consumer prices for each of the 19 household types into the 2001–02 HIES. Table 5.4 lists the 19 households in the SAM and the corresponding household characteristics of the 19 household groups in the HIES. We apply the average change in income of households h1–h19 from the model to all households belonging to the same group to arrive at a new column of income for those households. Similarly we apply the average change in consumer price of households h1–h19 from the model to the poverty line to arrive at a new poverty line for the group. With the new columns of household income and poverty line, we calculate the change in the poverty index.[2] We calculate poverty indexes for all Pakistan, urban, and rural households as summary statistics.

---

[2]Poverty impacts are measured by variations in FGT indexes with respect to their 2001–02 values. The FGT poverty measure is $P_\alpha = \frac{1}{n}\sum_{i=1}^{q}\left(\frac{z-y_i}{z}\right)^\alpha$, where n is population size, q is the number of people below the poverty line, y_i is income, and z is the poverty line. The poverty line is equal to the food poverty line plus the nonfood poverty line, respectively representing the estimated cost of basic food and nonfood requirements. The poverty headcount index, which measures the proportion of the population whose income (or consumption) falls below the poverty line, is obtained when $\alpha = 0$. When $\alpha = 1$, we obtain the poverty gap, which measures the depth of poverty, that is, how far the poor are below the poverty line on average. The poverty severity index is obtained when $\alpha = 2$. This measure is sensitive to the distribution among the poor, as more weight is given to the poorest below the poverty line.

CHAPTER 7

Definition of Policy Simulation Scenarios

The objective of this report is to analyze the intersectoral and poverty implications of key international and domestic economic changes that could affect the competitiveness of the cotton, yarn, and textile industries in Pakistan. We have designed four sets of simulation scenarios, and the definition of each one is given here.

SIM 1: Increase in Foreign Savings

After the 9/11 attacks in the United States, Pakistan experienced a surge in foreign exchange. In the period between 2001–02 and 2004–05, net inflows of foreign exchange increased by 111 percent (Government of Pakistan 2006a). This created pressure on the exchange rate, which appreciated by 12 percent (Table 7.1). Since the cotton-textile sectors are the major export earner, providing 60 percent of the total export receipts of the country, the impact on their performance could be substantial. In this simulation we analyze the effects of a 100 percent increase in foreign savings. We introduce this shock into the model by increasing the exogenous current account balance variable, which is *CAB* in equation (39) in Appendix A. This simulation scenario analyzes the impact of prices of tradables and nontradables and the corresponding changes in output. Factor prices, factor income, and household welfare and poverty are also assessed.

SIM 2: Increase in World Cotton and Textile Prices

As described previously, world cotton prices fluctuate significantly. The sharpest and most sustained drop in prices took place between 1994 and 2001, with COTLOOK B dropping by 57.8 percent. The declines in cotton yarn and cotton fabric prices during this period were much less, at 27.4 percent and 6.4 percent, respectively. Instead of a price drop, this simulation scenario considers an increase in cotton prices. We assume that the world price of cotton yarn increases by 20 percent. Using the ratios in Table 2.9 computed for the period 1994–2001, this implies a 42.6 percent increase in COTLOOK B and a 4.6 percent increase in the world price of cotton fabric. We rounded up the increase in the world price of cotton fabric to 5 percent.

Furthermore, in the analysis, we are constrained to implement this experiment by increasing the exogenous world price of cotton lint and yarn exports and imports (sector 20) using the increase in the world price of cotton yarn, and increasing the exogenous world price of textiles (sector 21) using the increase in the world price of cotton fabric. We increase both the *Pwm* in equation (40) and *Pwe* in equation (41) in Appendix A for only these two sectors. The first-round impact on export supply is captured in equation (36) through *Pe,* the domestic price of its export in local currency. However, in the succeeding adjustments, *D,* domestic demand, and *Pl,* local price, will affect the export supply of cotton lint and yarn as both are endogenous

Table 7.1 Change in exchange rate and prices (percent)

Years	Change in nominal Pakistan exchange rate	Pakistan inflation rate	U.S. inflation rate	Inflation-adjusted change in Pakistan exchange rate
2000–01	12.9	4.4	2.8	11.3
2001–02	5.1	3.5	1.6	3.1
2002–03	–4.8	3.1	2.3	–5.6
2003–04	–1.6	4.6	2.7	–3.5
2004–05	3.0	9.3	3.4	–2.9

Sources: Government of Pakistan (2006a) and http://inflationdata.com (for U.S. inflation rate).

variables. Similarly the impact of higher Pwm will channel through the import price equation and the import demand function in equation (38). Furthermore the curvature of the import demand and the export supply as indicated by the level of the elasticity of substitution, which are fixed, will influence the size of the effect.

To better understand the results of this experiment, we conduct three separate runs: SIM 2a, in which a 20 percent increase in the world price of cotton lint and yarn is simulated; SIM 2b, in which a 5 percent increase in the world price of textiles is simulated; and SIM 2c, in which both price increases are introduced simultaneously.

SIM 3: Increase in Production Subsidy

The textile industry in Pakistan is backed by a strong industry association, which enjoys a close relationship with the government and lobbies for government support. Substantial resources have been channeled to the spinning and weaving industries by suppressing raw cotton prices or through direct subsidies. In contrast, cotton farmers do not have such strong representation. This simulation provides analytics relevant to the debate over government subsidies to the industry.

Figure 7.1 illustrates a simple economics of a production subsidy. The supply curve is S(*Ps*) and the demand curve D(*Pd*). The initial equilibrium is at point (Q*, P*). With subsidy, the supply curve shifts to ES(*Pd*). The equilibrium quantity that is exchanged with subsidy is Qsub. The equilibrium price that consumers pay is *Pd*, while the price which producers receive is *Ps*. The rate of subsidy per unit is *Ps* – *Pd*. Therefore, in the equilibrium with subsidy, the quantity that is produced is consumed. Both producer and consumer surplus will improve. DWL is the value of providing to consumers who do not value the goods at more than its marginal cost. This amount is DWL = ½(Qsub – Q*)(*Ps* – *Pd*). The subsidy would involve cost to the government equivalent to (*Ps* – *Pd*)Qsub.

In our model we consider a production subsidy as a negative tax on output. We implement this through the output price equation (43) in Appendix A. The output price is $Px \cdot X \cdot (1+tx) = P1 \cdot d + Pe \cdot e$, where *tx* (negative) is a production subsidy. Since this will affect the indirect tax revenue of the government in equation (30), the following term will be added: $\sum Px \cdot X \cdot tx$. The indirect tax revenue, and therefore the total income of the government, declines if *tx* is implemented.

We implement a production subsidy in a manner that would not cause a government budget deficit. To do this we experiment with two compensatory tax measures: a general compensatory consumption tax, *nctx*, which is applied to all commodities, and a compensatory income tax,

Figure 7.1 Simple economics of a production subsidy

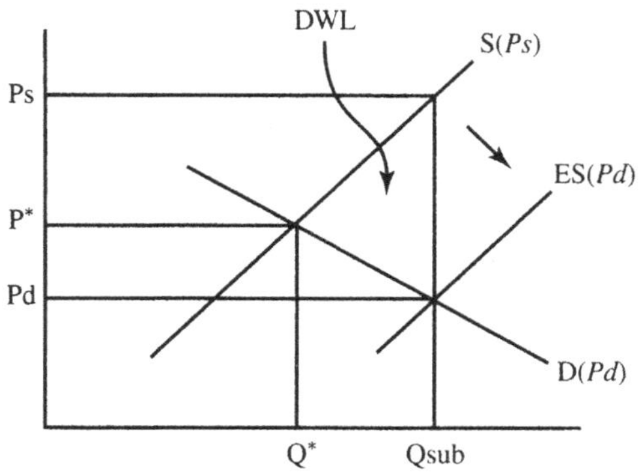

ndtxrh, which is applied to the urban nonpoor because all the rest of the household groups are untaxed (Table 5.4). These compensatory tax variables are solved endogenously in the model so that there is no net effect on the overall savings of the government.

To implement the compensatory consumption tax, we introduce *nctx* in equation (42) in the following way: $Pq \cdot Q = (1 + nctx)(Pd \cdot D + Pm \cdot M)$.[1] This will increase the consumer price of goods, but it will also generate additional government revenue that will offset whatever decline in government income may be due to the provision of a production subsidy and to reduction in other revenue because of changes in the variables in the revenue function of the government. Thus the following term is added to the indirect tax revenue of the government (equation 30): $\sum nctx\ (Pd \cdot D + Pm \cdot M)$.

On the other hand, to implement the compensatory income tax, *ndtxrh,* the disposable income of households in equation (26) will become $dyh = yh(1 - dtxrh[1 + ndtxrh])$. This will lower the disposable income of households, but it will generate additional revenue for the government that will offset the expenditure on the subsidy. The following term will be added to the direct income tax revenue of the government (equation 29): $\sum nctx\ (Pd \cdot D + Pm \cdot M)$.

SIM 4: Increase in Total Factor Productivity

As discussed earlier, recent studies on the cotton-textile sectors (Martin 2004; Altaf 2008; Salam 2008) have argued that improvement in productivity is one of the key challenges Pakistan faces in order to be competitive in the world markets for yarn and textiles. These international markets are expected to be more price responsive after the abolition of the MFA quotas. However, the liberalized market presents the greatest opportunities for those suppliers with high productivity. As Martin observes, for Pakistan raising productivity—by improving the efficiency of the production process or increasing the range and quality of the products produced—is key to reaping benefits from the abolition of the MFA.

The productivity simulations examine the effects of TFP improvement in the cotton-textile sectors. We conduct three separate experiments in which we increase TFP by 5 percent in raw cotton (sector 5; SIM 4a); raw cotton and cotton lint and yarn (sectors 5 and 20; SIM 4b); and raw cotton, cotton lint and yarn, and textiles (sectors 5, 20, and 21; SIM 4c). Improvement in TFP is incorporated by increasing the scale parameter, κ, in the relevant production function in equations (2) and (3) in Appendix A.

The effects of improvement in TFP have long-term implications. Thus we extend our CGE into a dynamic-recursive model to capture the economywide effects over time. A full description of the dynamic-recursive model is given in Appendix A. In the experiments we establish a baseline solution

[1]Generally, if *tx* is negative, *nctx* will be positive (or vice versa). However, they are not equal, because *nctx* is a general consumption tax while *tx* is specific to a sector. In addition, *nctx* will accommodate changes in other sources of government income as a result of the general equilibrium effects of implementing *tx*.

in which we assume labor supply to grow by 2 percent per year.[2] Sectoral capital stock, which is fixed within the year, will change in the following period depending on sectoral investment and depreciation. Sectoral investment depends on the rate of sectoral return to capital. There are higher investment flows into the sector if it has a relatively higher rate of return to capital. However, in the long run the sectoral variances in the rates of return to capital will drop, equalizing rates of investment. Furthermore the analysis in the previous scenarios incorporates the assumption that land use in agriculture is fixed. In the dynamic analysis we relax this assumption, allowing land to shift among crops.

With these assumptions we solve the model over the period 2001–27. This provides the baseline solution. To analyze the effects of higher productivity, we increase TFP starting in 2008 together with the assumptions in the baseline solution. The production scale parameter is increased in 2008 and retained it at this higher level until 2027. We then solve the model again and compare the new solution with the baseline. This exercise yields insights into the dynamic effects of productivity improvement over a 20-year period, 2008–27.

[2]This figure is based on the declining population growth rate in Pakistan: 2.6 percent in 1990–95, 2.3 percent in 1995–2000, and 1.9 percent in 2001–06 (Asian Development Bank 2007).

CHAPTER 8

Results of the Simulation Analysis

This chapter begins with a summary of the complete results of SIM 1. The discussion focuses on macroeconomic, sectoral, and household effects through changes in output and factor prices. The rest of the simulations are discussed under three topics: world price increases, increases in government subsidies, and improvements in TFP. For each simulation we present the macroeconomic, sectoral, and household effects. However, in the sectoral analysis we emphasize only the impact on the cotton, yarn, and textile sectors. The effects on the other sectors are relatively small for the shocks introduced in SIM 2 through SIM 4, and thus they are not extensively covered in the tables and text.

Increase in Foreign Savings

The objective of this experiment is to analyze the economywide effects of increased inflows of foreign savings into Pakistan. As discussed earlier, the period 2001–02 and 2004–05 saw net inflows of foreign exchange increasing by 111 percent; this put pressure on the exchange rate, which in turn appreciated by 12 percent. This had a significant impact on the cotton-textile sectors because they are major export earners, accounting for 60 percent of the country's total exports.

In the experiment, we analyze the effects of a 100 percent increase in foreign savings. In Table 8.1, foreign savings increase by Rs 135.67 billion. This results in a 23.24 percent increase in overall real investment. The significant increase in the inflow of foreign savings results in 9.51 percent appreciation of the real exchange rate, which in turn depresses real exports by 11 percent and pulls real imports up by 9 percent.[1] Overall real consumption increases by 1.33 percent. The composite price declines by 1.95 percent, the overall household consumer price index (CPI) declines by 1.69 percent, and domestic prices decline marginally by 0.63 percent.[2] The overall government balance deteriorates by Rs 1.45 billion due to the reduction in tariff revenue because of the appreciation of the exchange rate and the reduction in the average returns to land, as described later.[3] In Table 5.6 one source of government revenue is water (7.2 percent of total revenue), which in the model is considered a part of land.

[1]Real exchange rate appreciation is the change in the nominal exchange rate, which is also the change in the real exchange rate because the model considers Pindex (the weighted sectoral price of value added) as constant and the nominal exchange rate as variable in the closure. This is the measure of the change in real exchange rate that is used in the rest of the simulations.

[2]Composite price is the weighted average of import price and domestic price. Household consumer price is the consumption-weighted composite price. Domestic price includes indirect taxes.

[3]One source of government revenue is income from water, which we consider another form of land in the model.

The intersectoral results are presented in Table 8.2. The highest positive impact is on the construction sector, which is a non-tradable sector with zero exports and imports. Its overall output improves by 8.78 percent, and its output price improves by 13.47 percent. It is followed by the cement and bricks sector, which supplies much of the material requirements of the construction sector. Its output improves by 3.74 percent and its output price by 48.32 percent. Output of the private services sector improves by 1.26 percent. However, there are negative effects on cotton, yarn, and textiles. The output of the textile sector declines by 7.67 percent; that of the cotton lint and yarn sector, by 5.83 percent; and that of the raw cotton sector, by 5.13 percent. The largest drop is in the leather industry, where output declines by 11.37 percent. The "other food" sector registers a drop of 5.05 percent. There are negative effects on the rice sector, on both paddy and rice milling, but there is a slight positive effect on wheat and sugar.

There is significant movement of labor across sectors. Employment of skilled and unskilled labor in the cement and bricks sector improves by 43.85 and 43.14 percent, respectively. In the construction sector, employment of skilled labor improves by 13.53 percent while that of unskilled labor improves by 11.87 percent. Employment also improves in the private services sector. Labor moves largely from the leather, other food, cotton, yarn, textile, and rice sectors.

Exports of all sectors decline because of the appreciation of the real exchange rate. The largest drop is in the cement and bricks sector because of high domestic demand. There is also a substantial drop in exports of leather. Exports of cotton lint and yarn and of textiles fall by 4.36 percent and 16.85 percent, respectively. Conversely the appreciation of the exchange rate results in higher sectoral import demand in all sectors except cotton lint and yarn. Imports of yarn decline because output of the textile sector, the user of yarn, falls.

Table 8.1 Macro effects: SIM 1, increase in foreign savings

Variables	Change from base (%)
Real consumption	1.33
Real investment	23.24
Real exports	–11.03
Real imports	9.00
Real exchange rate	–9.51
Export prices	–9.51
Import prices	–9.50
Household consumer price index[a]	–1.69
Composite price	–1.95
Domestic prices	–0.63
Price of investment	1.81
	Amount (billion Rs)
Government balance	–1.45
Total government income	–1.45
Tariff revenue	–0.87
Indirect tax revenue	1.42
Direct tax revenue	0.34
Other revenue	–2.33
Total household savings	–0.47
Foreign savings	135.67
Firm savings	0.00
Overall savings[b]	133.76

[a]Composite price weighted by consumption expenditure.

[b]Sum of government balance, total household savings, foreign savings, and firm savings.

The generally negative effects on agricultural and other traded goods and the positive effects on the construction-related and service sectors result in differentiated effects on factor prices. In Table 8.3 the impacts on the wages of farm labor and on the average returns to land are both negative in real and nominal terms. In real terms the wages of farm labor drop by 6.97 percent, while the average returns to land drop by

Table 8.2 Intersectoral effects: SIM 1, increase in foreign savings (percent change from base)

Commodities	Output		Labor				Exports		Imports	
	Volume	Price	Skilled	Unskilled	Investment	Returns to capital	Volume	Price	Volume	Price
Raw cotton	−5.13	−9.70	—	−15.33	−13.60	−13.61	—	—	—	—
Cotton lint and yarn	−5.83	−9.56	−23.02	−23.87	−27.68	−20.96	−4.36	−9.51	−8.37	−9.50
Textiles	−7.67	−9.13	−25.41	−26.23	−31.62	−23.14	−16.85	−9.51	16.31	−9.50
Wheat, irrigated	0.16	−5.80	—	0.47	1.43	−6.39	−4.74	−9.51	3.52	−9.51
Wheat, nonirrigated	0.43	−5.46	—	1.25	3.54	−5.43	—	—	—	—
Paddy, IRRI	−1.73	−12.46	—	−9.65	−23.59	−18.75	—	—	—	—
Paddy, basmati	−0.88	−12.09	—	−8.37	−20.66	−17.21	—	—	—	—
Sugarcane	0.52	−3.66	—	4.11	11.54	−1.84	—	—	—	—
Other major crops	−0.61	−7.15	—	−1.74	−4.41	−9.13	−3.75	−9.51	1.46	−9.51
Fruits and vegetables	0.55	−3.51	—	2.82	7.89	−3.46	−7.21	−9.51	6.00	−9.51
Livestock, cattle, and dairy	0.19	0.04	—	1.90	23.46	3.28	−11.61	−9.51	8.02	−9.51
Poultry	0.31	0.61	—	3.14	27.50	4.95	−12.14	−9.51	—	—
Forestry	−0.54	−8.38	—	−2.65	0.00	0.00	−2.06	−9.51	1.50	−9.51
Fishing industry	−1.74	−3.91	—	−5.63	0.60	−6.78	−8.84	−9.51	6.38	−9.51
Agriculture	**−0.21**	**−2.88**	**—**	**−1.25**	**20.63**	**2.02**	**−6.26**	**−9.51**	**5.02**	**−9.51**
Agriculture, excluding raw cotton	**0.08**	**−2.48**	**—**	**0.39**	**20.99**	**2.18**	**−6.26**	**−9.51**	**5.02**	**−9.51**
Mining	−0.86	−2.52	−2.71	−3.43	7.00	−3.86	−11.32	−9.51	6.08	−9.51
Vegetable oil	−0.91	−4.02	−6.35	−7.72	5.50	−4.53	−11.92	−9.51	8.25	−9.50
Wheat milling	0.61	−3.08	3.85	2.33	21.09	2.28	−12.29	−9.51	11.96	−9.50
Rice milling, IRRI	−2.80	−7.52	−12.14	−13.43	−3.11	−8.51	−6.93	−9.51	—	—
Rice milling, basmati	−1.14	−6.41	−4.66	−6.05	8.05	−3.39	−7.56	−9.51	—	—
Sugar	0.57	−1.03	2.91	1.40	19.62	1.66	−15.91	−9.51	15.05	−9.51
Other food	−5.05	−7.43	−26.20	−27.28	−23.21	−18.55	−9.26	−9.51	6.25	−9.50
Leather	−11.37	−2.58	−38.76	−39.66	−40.13	−28.08	−23.53	−9.51	16.37	−9.51
Wood products	0.22	−1.49	0.78	0.29	18.78	1.30	−15.42	−9.51	13.92	−9.50
Chemicals	−1.41	−6.20	−6.27	−6.73	−11.14	−12.38	−8.24	−9.51	1.98	−9.50
Cement and bricks	3.74	48.32	43.85	43.14	392.97	106.36	−61.39	−9.51	—	—
Petroleum refining	−0.80	−4.83	−2.92	−3.40	2.27	−6.01	—	—	1.73	−9.51
Other manufacturing	0.28	−3.02	1.17	0.67	20.61	2.08	−12.69	−9.51	11.80	−9.50

(continued)

Table 8.2 Continued

Commodities	Output		Labor		Investment	Returns to capital	Exports		Imports	
	Volume	Price	Skilled	Unskilled			Volume	Price	Volume	Price
Energy	–0.70	–5.71	–3.32	–3.80	0.59	–6.78	—	—	—	0.00
Construction	8.78	13.47	13.53	11.87	36.36	8.54	—	—	—	0.00
Industry	**–1.68**	**–2.13**	**–2.98**	**1.72**	**28.50**	**0.39**	**–12.86**	**–9.51**	**8.76**	**–9.50**
Industry, excluding yarn and textiles	**0.62**	**0.87**	**3.79**	**5.08**	**45.60**	**7.03**	**–11.51**	**–9.51**	**8.76**	**–9.50**
Commerce	–0.69	–0.10	–0.59	–1.08	12.45	–1.44	–5.48	–9.51	21.06	–9.51
Transportation	–0.08	–2.27	0.78	–0.45	16.59	0.36	–3.85	–9.51	0.00	0.00
Housing	0.00	5.37	0.00	0.00	27.46	4.93	0.00	0.00	0.00	0.00
Private services	1.26	0.52	4.18	2.91	22.94	3.06	–3.93	–9.51	15.47	–9.51
Public services	1.10	–1.08	1.10	0.00	0.00	—	0.00	0.00	—	0.00
Services	**0.36**	**–0.26**	**1.05**	**0.07**	**20.01**	**1.80**	**–3.86**	**–9.51**	**15.70**	**–9.51**
Total	**–0.54**	**–1.50**	**0.00**	**–0.01**	**23.24**	**1.40**	**–11.03**	**–9.51**	**9.00**	**–9.50**

Table 8.3 Factor price effects: SIM 1, increase in foreign savings (percent change from base)

Factor prices	Real[a]	Nominal
Skilled labor	1.42	-0.27
Unskilled farm labor	-6.97	-8.66
Unskilled workers	2.41	0.72
Average returns to capital	3.09	1.40
Average returns to land	-5.59	-7.27

[a]Less change in consumer price index.

Table 8.4 Real income effects: SIM 1, increase in foreign savings (percent)

Household groups	Real income change from base	Population distribution
Pakistan overall	1.31	—
Urban	1.85	28.6
Urban poor	2.27	8.1
Rural	0.73	71.4
Farmers[a]	-0.41	34.2
Workers[b]	2.39	6.6
Other rural households[c]	2.40	30.7
Other rural poor households	2.66	16.8

Note: See Table 5.4 for definitions of the household groups.
[a]Large, medium, small, and landless in Punjab, Sindh, and other Pakistan.
[b]Landless agricultural workers in Punjab, Sindh, and other Pakistan.
[c]Nonfarm rural households.

5.59 percent.[4] There are increases of 2.41 percent in the wages of unskilled workers, 1.42 percent in the wages of skilled labor, and 3.09 percent in the average returns to capital, because the construction-related and service sectors use substantial amounts of these factors.

Table 8.5 Poverty effects: SIM 1, increase in foreign savings (percent change from base)

Poverty index	Pakistan	Urban	Rural
Poverty headcount	-6.63	-7.41	-6.38
Poverty gap	-8.20	-8.87	-8.01
Poverty severity	-9.88	-10.27	-9.76

There are 19 household groups in the model, but in the presentation of household results we aggregate them into the seven broader groups shown in Table 8.4. Overall household income improves by 1.31 percent. There are relatively more positive effects on urban households—especially on the urban poor, who constitute 8.1 percent of the population—than on rural households. Among rural households, rural farmers are negatively affected. They make up 34.2 percent of the population. These effects are largely due to the negative effects on prices of factors owned by these groups. However, there are positive income effects on both rural workers and other rural households. This is because of positive factor price effects, the movement of unskilled labor across sectors, and high growth in the construction-related and service sectors, which employ a substantial amount of unskilled labor.

The effects on poverty as evaluated by the microsimulation analysis are presented in Table 8.5. The overall poverty headcount index drops by 6.63 percent. There is a relatively greater drop in the urban poverty headcount index than in the rural headcount index. This is due to the negative real income effects among rural poor farmers. However, for Pakistan as a whole as well as in both urban and rural areas, there is a greater drop in the poverty gap and severity indexes. This is due to the larger increase in

[4]This causes government income from land (water) to drop.

real income of the urban poor (8.1 percent of the population), rural poor agricultural laborers (3.6 percent of the population), and rural poor non-farmers (18.1 percent of the population).

The foregoing analysis captures the effects of a capital inflow in the generally stable economic and political environment of 2001–05. However, these gains may be undermined by recent unfavorable developments, including the rise in world commodity prices (such as those for food and oil) and the political uncertainty stemming from the firing of Supreme Court judges, the assassination of the former prime minister, and the fall of the Musharraf administration.

The surge in world commodity prices translated into higher consumer prices in Pakistan. The overall annual inflation rate increased from 6.5 percent in August 2007 to 24.3 percent in July 2008 (State Bank of Pakistan 2008). Over the same period the food inflation rate increased from 8.6 percent to 33.8 percent. The Pakistan rupee depreciated nominally against the U.S. dollar from the 2007 average of Rs 60.7 to Rs 76.5 per U.S. dollar in September 2008. However, because of the higher rate of domestic inflation, the real effective exchange rate index appreciated from 96.8 in August 2007 to 91.1 in May 2008.

Because of higher commodity prices, the current account deficit ballooned from about US$5 billion in the 2005–06 fiscal year to US$14 billion in 2007–08 (State Bank of Pakistan 2008). This is despite the sustained inflow of workers' remittances, which increased from US$10.7 billion in 2005–06 to US$11.6 billion in 2007–08. The financing of the huge current account deficit came from three sources: the sustained inflow of foreign direct investment despite the political uncertainty (from US$3.45 billion in 2005–06 to US$5 billion in 2007–08), increased proceeds from loans (from US$1.7 billion in 2006–07 to US$2.4 billion in 2007–08), and a drawdown in official reserves of US$5.9 billion in 2007–08. Portfolio investment was a major source of current account financing in 2006–07, with a net inflow of US$3.3 billion. However, because of the present political turmoil it dried up in the 2007–08 fiscal year.

If the current account deficit continues to widen because of high world commodity prices and the political crisis remains unresolved, both foreign direct investment and proceeds from loans may dry up as well. A huge drawdown of the limited official reserves may not be sustainable in the long run. If this happens a balance-of-payments crisis may become a real possibility. This will have an unfavorable effect on real sector growth and therefore on poverty. While the real sector is still registering respectable growth (GDP growth of 5.78 percent in 2007–08), there are signs of an economic downturn (Government of Pakistan 2008). The growth of the agricultural sector decelerated from 6.3 percent in 2005–06 to 1.49 percent in 2007–08. There has also been a significant deceleration in the growth of the manufacturing sector over the same period. However, the growth of the services sector is still robust at 8.16 percent in 2007–08.

Increases in World Cotton and Textile Prices

As discussed previously, world cotton prices fluctuate widely. The early 1990s saw a sharp hike in cotton prices until 1994, then a significant drop until 2001. During these years, international cotton prices (the COTLOOK A and B indexes) fell nearly 60 percent, while U.S. cotton prices fell by 40 percent. Wide swings in cotton prices have continued since 2002. After a recovery in 2002 and 2003, prices dropped again in 2004. The past three years have seen improvement in prices. Since cotton is a major crop in Pakistan, wide price fluctuations could have significant economywide effects. In analyzing this scenario, we separately simulate a 20 percent increase in the world price of cotton

Table 8.6 Macro effects: SIM 2, increase in world cotton and textile prices

Variables	SIM 2a	SIM 2b	SIM 2c
		Change from base (%)	
Real consumption	0.25	0.43	0.62
Real investment	0.63	–0.14	0.49
Real exports	–1.62	–0.23	–1.52
Real imports	0.61	0.89	1.40
Real exchange rate	–1.88	–3.24	–4.84
Export prices	–0.12	–1.70	–1.61
Import prices	–1.73	–3.16	–4.62
Household consumer price index[a]	–0.26	–0.57	–0.80
Composite price	0.10	–0.90	–0.74
Domestic price	0.42	–0.52	–0.07
Price of investment	–1.18	–1.98	–2.99
		Amount (billion Rs)	
Government balance	1.29	–5.79	–4.02
Total government income	1.29	–5.79	–4.02
Tariff revenue	–0.02	–0.99	–0.98
Indirect tax revenue	0.34	–4.23	–3.37
Direct tax revenue	–1.40	0.33	–1.11
Other revenue	2.37	–0.89	1.44
Total household savings	–1.12	–0.08	–1.27
Foreign savings	–3.15	–5.43	–8.11
Firm savings	0.0	0.0	0.0
Overall savings[b]	–2.97	–11.30	–13.40

Note: SIM 2a, 20 percent increase in world prices of cotton lint and yarn; SIM 2b, 5 percent increase in world prices of textiles; SIM 2c, combination of SIM 2a and 2b.
[a]Composite price weighted by consumption expenditure.
[b]Sum of government balance, total household savings, foreign savings, and firm savings.

lint and yarn (SIM 2a), a 5 percent increase in the world price of textiles (SIM 2b), and a combined price increase for both products (SIM 2c).

The macro results are presented in Table 8.6. In all three cases there is appreciation of the real exchange rate. The exchange rate appreciates by 1.88 percent in SIM 2a and 3.24 percent in SIM 2b. Although the world price of cotton yarn under SIM 2a increases more than the world price of textiles under SIM 2b, the effect of the latter increase is larger than that of the former because the textile sector has a much larger share of total export receipts in the 2001–02 SAM (31.9 percent versus 9.0 percent in Table 5.1). The impact on the sector's exports is positive (for example, exports increase 50.1 percent for cotton lint and yarn in SIM 2a and 6.8 percent for textiles in SIM 2b in Table 8.7, as discussed subsequently). However, with constant foreign savings in foreign currency at the initial benchmark level in the simulations, appreciation of the real exchange rate decreases overall exports and increases overall imports.[5]

Under SIM 2a, government revenue improves by Rs 1.29 billion despite the reduction in tariff revenue (due to the appreciation of the exchange rate) and the drop in direct income tax revenue (due to declining rates of return to capital and wages of skilled and unskilled labor, which affect household income, as discussed later). This is because there is relatively higher average return to land, which is a source of government revenue. Moreover, the drop in foreign savings by Rs 3.15 billion is due to the appreciation of the exchange rate. There is also a drop of Rs 1.12 billion in household savings.[6] Thus overall savings drop by Rs 2.97 billion. The price of investment drops by 1.18 percent.[7] Therefore, despite the drop in overall nominal savings (nominal investment), real investment improves marginally by 0.63 percent.

Under SIM 2b, because of higher appreciation of the exchange rate of 3.24 percent, there is a larger drop in tariff revenue and indirect tax revenue.[8] This leads to a greater reduction in government savings. There is a relatively lower drop in nominal household savings compared with SIM 2a. In addition, due to the higher appreciation of the exchange rate, foreign savings in domestic currency drop by Rs 5.43 billion. Thus overall savings drop by Rs 11.3 billion. There is a corresponding larger drop in the price of investment by 1.98 percent. This is not enough to offset the overall drop in nominal savings (nominal investment). Thus real investment drops marginally by 0.14 percent.

Under SIM 2c the macro effects are larger because the 20 percent increase in the world price of cotton yarn and the 5 percent increase in the world price of cotton fabric are simulated simultaneously. However, the combined effects are not the simple sum of the individual effects under SIM 2a and SIM 2b.

The increase in the government deficit under SIM 2c is lower than in SIM 2b because of the increase in other revenue due to the increase in the returns to land, and because of the smaller reduction in revenue from indirect taxes despite the higher appreciation of the exchange rate because of higher import volume. Overall savings decline in SIM 2c more than in SIM 2b. However, there is more of a reduction in the price of investment (2.99 percent); thus the net effect on real investment is an improvement of 0.49 percent. Exports decline because of the appreciation of the exchange rate, while imports increase. There is more of a decline in the household CPI in SIM 2c.

The intersectoral effects of the price shocks are shown in Table 8.7. The export and import prices of cotton lint and yarn increase by 17.75 percent under SIM 2a, which translates to a 16.43 percent increase in its output price and a 15.82 percent increase in its domestic price.[9] This makes the export market relatively more profitable than the domestic market; thus exports increase relative to domestic sales. Exports

---

[5]Foreign savings in domestic currency drop because of the appreciation of the exchange rate.

[6]These balances are in nominal values. However, we shall see later in the analysis that the real household income effects are positive, which implies that the effect on real household savings is also positive.

[7]The price of investment is given in equation (46) in Appendix A.

[8]Note that in equation (30) in Appendix A the indirect tax revenue is also affected by fluctuations in the exchange rate. When imported goods enter the domestic market, indirect taxes are imposed on them in the same way as on domestically produced goods.

[9]The figure of 17.75 percent is based on $Pe = Pwe \cdot er$. In differential form, this can be expressed as $\Delta Pe = (Pwe \cdot \Delta er) + (\Delta Pwe \cdot er) + (\Delta Pwe \cdot \Delta er)$. Both Pwe and er are originally 1.

increase by 50.15 percent while domestic demand decreases by 0.55 percent. The output increase of 13.27 percent is therefore driven by the increase in exports. This higher output increases the rates of return to capital relative to the other sectors. Thus investment in the cotton lint and yarn sector increases by 156.02 percent. Since the increase in the domestic price for cotton lint and yarn is lower than the increase in the corresponding import price (15.82 percent versus 17.74 percent), the relative price change results in lower imports of cotton lint and yarn.

The world price shock for cotton lint and yarn has major intersectoral effects on the raw cotton and textile sectors. The textile sector buys from the domestic yarn sector and also purchases imported yarn. From the input side, as both sources decline, the output of the textile sector drops by 8.61 percent and its capital returns by 26.16 percent. The drop in its export price (1.88 percent) is higher than the drop in its domestic price (1.33 percent). Thus there is a greater decline in its exports (16.19 percent) compared with its domestic demand (3.64 percent). From the demand side the drop in domestic demand and exports results in lower output for the textile sector.

The impact on raw cotton is different. Since the raw cotton sector does not sell to the export market and its major buyer is the domestic cotton lint and yarn sector, there is a demand pull effect from the 13.27 percent increase in the output of the latter. The effect on its output price is an increase of 13.02 percent, which is somewhat less than the 16.43 percent increase in the output price of cotton lint and yarn. Output of raw cotton improves by 11.75 percent. This effect improves the returns to factors used in raw cotton production. The returns to land and capital improve by 27.16 percent. Higher returns to capital increase investment by 64.37 percent.

Under SIM 2b, a 5 percent increase in the world price of cotton fabric translates to a 1.6 percent increase in the domestic export and import prices of textiles. Since the increase in domestic price is only 1.39 percent, this leads to a 6.8 percent increase in exports. This growth is higher than the 1.48 percent improvement in domestic demand, which results primarily from relatively lower prices for domestic textiles compared with imports. The output of the textile sector improves by 3.59 percent, largely because of increased exports. The rates of return to capital improve by 12.56 percent, which increases investment by 25.3 percent.

The intersectoral impact of higher world prices of cotton fabric is different from the effects of higher world prices of cotton yarn. Because of the appreciation of the exchange rate, the import price of yarn drops by 3.24 percent. This leads to imports that are higher by 14.16 percent. The increase in domestic demand for cotton lint and yarn is only 1.23 percent—not enough to meet the 3.59 percent growth of the textile industry without the increased imports.

The appreciation of the exchange rate also leads to exports of yarn that are lower by 10.24 percent. The increase of 1.23 percent in domestic demand for yarn is not enough to offset the drop in exports. Thus the output of lint and yarn drops by 1.87 percent, which in turn results in a 1.66 percent decline in the domestic demand for raw cotton. The output of raw cotton drops by the same amount because it does not trade internationally.

The drop in output of cotton lint and yarn decreases the rates of return to sectoral capital by 6.62 percent. Thus investment in the sector drops by 13.75 percent. Similarly the drop in output of raw cotton leads to declining rates of return to capital and land. Thus investment in the sector drops by 10.35 percent.

Under SIM 2c, in which both higher world prices of cotton lint and yarn and higher prices of textiles are incorporated simultaneously, whenever the results of SIM 2a and SIM 2b are of the same sign, the results under SIM 2c will be larger in

Table 8.7 Intersectoral effects: SIM 2, increase in world cotton and textile prices (percent change from base)

	Output		Domestic demand			Exports		Imports		Returns to:	
Commodities	Output	Output price	Domestic demand	Domestic price (including indirect tax)	Investment	Exports	Export price in local currency	Imports	Import price in local currency	Capital	Land
	SIM 2a: 20% increase in world prices of cotton lint and yarn										
Raw cotton	11.75	13.02	11.75	13.01	64.37	—	—	—	—	27.16	27.16
Lint and yarn	13.27	16.43	–0.55	15.82	156.20	50.15	17.75	–34.13	17.74	58.76	—
Textiles	–8.61	–1.54	–3.64	–1.33	–44.58	–16.19	–1.88	10.79	–1.87	–26.16	—
Agriculture	0.32	2.58	0.43	2.67	2.11	–5.31	–1.88	3.23	–1.88	0.17	7.42
Excluding raw cotton	–0.35	1.97	–0.25	2.05	1.46	–5.31	–1.88	3.23	–1.88	–0.11	5.00
Industry	–0.94	0.65	–0.76	0.71	1.22	–1.72	0.36	0.46	–1.72	–1.95	—
Excluding lint and yarn, and textiles	–0.40	–0.64	–0.17	–0.44	–2.87	–1.82	–1.88	0.55	–1.87	–2.27	—
Services	0.07	–0.96	0.08	–0.92	–0.46	–0.36	–1.88	1.63	–1.88	–1.04	—
Total	–0.27	0.37	–0.12	0.42	0.63	–1.62	–0.12	0.61	–1.73	–1.06	7.42

	SIM 2b: 5% increase in world prices of textiles										
Raw cotton	–1.66	–3.32	–1.66	–3.32	–10.35	—	—	—	—	–4.79	–4.79
Lint and yarn	–1.87	–2.89	1.23	–2.78	–13.75	–10.24	–3.24	14.16	–3.24	–6.62	—
Textiles	3.59	1.48	1.48	1.39	25.30	6.80	1.60	–3.57	1.60	12.56	—
Agriculture	–0.06	–1.09	–0.02	–1.05	–0.21	–2.00	–3.24	1.54	–3.24	0.44	–2.78
Excluding raw cotton	0.03	–0.96	0.07	–0.91	–0.11	–2.00	–3.24	1.54	–3.24	0.49	–2.53
Industry	0.19	–0.93	0.23	–0.84	–0.27	0.05	–1.28	0.69	–3.15	0.22	—
Excluding lint and yarn, and textiles	–0.57	–1.40	–0.14	–1.11	–4.31	–3.20	–3.24	0.66	–3.24	–1.70	—
Services	–0.01	–0.14	0.04	–0.00	–0.02	–1.11	–3.24	3.97	–3.24	0.54	—
Total	0.06	–0.63	0.09	–0.52	–0.14	–0.23	–1.70	0.89	–3.16	0.42	–2.78
	SIM 2c: combination of SIM 2a and 2b										
Raw cotton	10.05	9.48	10.05	9.48	49.46	—	—	—	—	21.57	21.57
Lint and yarn	11.36	13.22	1.35	12.79	126.44	38.08	14.19	–25.61	14.19	49.64	—
Textiles	–4.36	0.08	–1.83	0.19	–24.94	–8.22	–0.08	5.00	–0.08	–13.85	—
Agriculture	0.26	1.44	0.40	1.56	2.17	–7.02	–4.84	4.63	–4.84	0.48	4.51
Excluding raw cotton	–0.32	0.96	–0.18	1.08	1.67	–7.02	–4.84	4.63	–4.84	0.26	2.43
Industry	–0.57	–0.17	–0.40	–0.04	–0.05	–1.28	–0.74	1.06	–4.60	–1.67	—
Excluding lint and yarn, and textiles	–0.91	–1.89	–0.28	–1.42	–5.93	–4.77	–4.84	1.20	–4.83	–3.63	—
Services	0.07	–1.06	0.13	–0.90	0.09	–1.39	–4.84	5.40	–4.84	–0.52	—
Total	–0.14	–0.22	0.01	–0.07	0.49	–1.52	–1.61	1.40	–4.62	–0.66	4.51

magnitude. If the results are of the opposite sign under SIM 2a and SIM 2b, the results under SIM 2c carry the sign of the larger effect, and the magnitude lies between the magnitudes of the two effects. For example, the output of the textile sector drops by 8.61 percent in SIM 2a but increases by 3.59 percent under SIM 2b. Since the effect under the first is larger than the result under the second, the result in SIM 2c is a drop in textile output.

The impacts on factor prices are presented in Table 8.8. SIM 2a generates favorable effects on the wages of farm labor and returns to land, factors used heavily in agriculture, particularly in the raw cotton sector. However, there is a decline in the wages of skilled labor, the wages of unskilled workers, and the average returns to capital. The impact on factor prices under SIM 2b, however, is the opposite, with a decline in the wages of farm labor and in the returns to land. If world prices of both yarn and textiles under SIM 2c are considered, there are positive effects on all real factor prices. However, under SIM 2c the appreciation of the exchange rate is higher (4.84 percent in Table 8.6). Since households receive 5.3 percent of their income from abroad (Table 5.5), as we shall discuss subsequently, an appreciation has negative effects on them despite the higher factor prices under this scenario.

Table 8.8 Factor price effects: SIM 2, increase in world cotton and textile prices (percent change from base)

Factor prices	Real[a]	Nominal
	SIM 2a	
Skilled labor	–0.45	–0.71
Unskilled farm labor	13.25	12.99
Unskilled workers	–0.26	–0.52
Average returns to capital	–0.80	–1.06
Average returns to land	7.68	7.42
	SIM 2b	
Skilled labor	1.13	0.56
Unskilled farm labor	–2.58	–3.15
Unskilled workers	0.47	–0.10
Average returns to capital	0.99	0.42
Average returns to land	–2.20	–2.78
	SIM 2c	
Skilled labor	0.56	–0.24
Unskilled farm labor	10.20	9.40
Unskilled workers	0.19	–0.61
Average returns to capital	0.13	–0.66
Average returns to land	5.31	4.51

Note: SIM 2a, 20 percent increase in world prices of cotton lint and yarn; SIM 2b, 5 percent increase in world prices of textiles; SIM 2c, combination of SIM 2a and 2b.

[a]Less change in consumer price index.

Table 8.9 shows that overall household real income improves by 0.25 percent under SIM 2a, 0.40 percent under SIM 2b, and 0.59 percent under SIM 2c. The impacts across household groups differ. In SIM 2a urban households are negatively affected. This is because of the decline in the wages of skilled labor, the wages of unskilled workers, and the average returns to capital. Rural workers and rural nonfarm households also have lower income because of the lower wages of unskilled workers. However, rural farmers benefit from the increase in the wages of farm labor and the average returns to land. In SIM 2b the decline in the wages of farm labor and the average returns to land result in lower income for farmers. The rest of the household groups realize higher income. In SIM 2c the income of the urban poor and rural non-farmers again declines. This is because of the appreciation of the exchange rate (4.84 percent), which negatively affects their income from abroad. Although they earn higher real return for the factors of production they supply, the increase is relatively smaller and the higher appreciation of the exchange rate in this scenario has larger negative effects on their overall income.

The impact on poverty is presented in Table 8.10. Overall poverty headcount

Table 8.9 Real income effects: SIM 2, increase in world cotton and textile prices (percent)

Household groups	Population distribution	Real income change from base		
		SIM 2a	SIM 2b	SIM 2c
Pakistan overall	—	0.25	0.40	0.59
Urban	28.6	–0.58	0.74	0.10
Urban poor	8.1	–0.58	0.33	–0.27
Rural	71.4	1.13	0.05	1.12
Farmers[a]	34.2	2.41	–0.31	2.00
Workers[b]	6.6	–0.87	0.45	–0.42
Other rural households[c]	30.7	–0.70	0.61	–0.12
Other rural poor households	16.8	–0.90	0.60	–0.32

Notes: SIM 2a, 20 percent increase in world prices of cotton lint and yarn; SIM 2b, 5 percent increase in world prices of textiles; SIM 2c, combination of SIM 2a and 2b. See Table 5.4 for definitions of the household groups.
[a]Large, medium, small, and landless in Punjab, Sindh, and other Pakistan.
[b]Landless agricultural workers in Punjab, Sindh, and other Pakistan.
[c]Nonfarm rural households.

in Pakistan declines by 0.8 percent under SIM 2a, mainly because of the 1.66 percent drop in the poverty index of rural households. The drop in rural poverty is attributed largely to the improvement in income of rural farmers. However, the smaller decline in the rural poverty gap and the slight increase in the rural poverty severity index are due to the decline in income of rural non-farmers, especially the poor within the group. In SIM 2b all poverty indexes decline; however, urban poverty incidence declines faster than rural poverty incidence. This is because rural farmers have declining income.

Under SIM 2c overall poverty incidence drops by 2.01 percent, faster than under the previous two scenarios. Urban poverty incidence has not changed. Both the urban poverty gap and the urban poverty severity index have increased because of the decline in income of the urban poor and of rural non-farmers, especially the poor within the group.

Because an increase in world cotton lint prices will have a particularly concentrated effect among cotton-producing households,

Table 8.10 Poverty effects: SIM 2, increase in world cotton and textile prices (percent change from base)

Poverty index	Pakistan	Urban	Rural
		SIM 2a	
Poverty headcount	–0.80	1.90	–1.66
Poverty gap	0.23	2.42	–0.42
Poverty severity	0.63	2.82	0.01
		SIM 2b	
Poverty headcount	–0.96	–1.23	–0.87
Poverty gap	–1.42	–1.32	–1.45
Poverty severity	–1.75	–1.53	–1.81
		SIM 2c	
Poverty headcount	–2.01	0.00	–2.65
Poverty gap	–1.12	1.10	–1.78
Poverty severity	–1.08	1.29	–1.76

Note: SIM 2a, 20 percent increase in world prices of cotton lint and yarn; SIM 2b, 5 percent increase in world prices of textiles; SIM 2c, combination of SIM 2a and 2b.

the disaggregation of poverty results between cotton and non-cotton households in Punjab, Sindh, and other Pakistan is discussed in Box 8.1. This additional disentangling of the results shown for rural Pakistan in Table 8.10 shows that a 20 percent increase in the world price of cotton lint will translate into a significant drop in poverty among cotton households.

Increase in Production Subsidy

As discussed in Chapter 3, the cotton, textile, and apparel industries in Pakistan are large. Of the three, the textile subsector has the dominant influence through its powerful industry association, the All Pakistan Textile Mills Association (Altaf 2008). It benefits from substantial government support through subsidies. Considerable resources have been channeled to the spinning and weaving industries by suppressing raw cotton prices. Cotton farmers have no comparably strong representation.

This section analyzes the effects of separately increasing production subsidies to textiles, cotton lint and yarn, and raw cotton. In conducting this experiment we hold government savings fixed. Fixing this variable requires us to incorporate a compensatory tax. The tax will automatically offset the government expenditure for the subsidy. We introduce two alternatives, a compensatory consumption tax and a compensatory income tax, and conduct a comparative analysis. The compensatory consumption tax increases consumer prices. Therefore the subsidy cum compensatory consumption tax will generate two opposing effects, and the net impact on poverty could either be positive or negative. The compensatory income tax will decrease the disposable income of households. However, Table 5.5 indicates that it is only the urban non-poor who are paying income tax. Thus the subsidy cum compensatory income tax generates reinforcing positive welfare effects on households outside the urban non-poor group. They will benefit from lower prices due to the subsidy and an income transfer from the urban non-poor through a higher income tax.

We conduct four experiments involving a 5 percent production subsidy. Three have a compensatory consumption tax and one has a compensatory income tax. SIM 3a applies the subsidy only to the textile sector; SIM 3b, only to the cotton lint and yarn sector; and SIM 3c, only to the raw cotton sector. SIM 3d applies the production subsidy only to the textile sector with a compensatory income tax.

If the subsidy is given to the textile industry (SIM 3a) and the compensatory consumption tax is imposed, the textile output price increases by 2.97 percent while the domestic price decreases by 2.28 percent (Table 8.11). Textile output improves by 5.67 percent. A relative price change favors exports over domestic demand and increases exports of textiles by 10 percent. Appreciation of the real exchange rate equals 2.01 percent. Because of its large share in total exports, the high export growth offsets a decline in exports in the rest of the sectors due to the appreciation of the real exchange rate.

Thus overall exports of the economy improve by 0.85 percent (Table 8.12). The appreciation also results in lower prices (export price, import price, composite price, consumer price, and price of investment) and foreign savings in domestic currency that are lower by Rs 3.37 billion.

The amount of subsidy to the textile sector is Rs 29.67 billion. The consumption tax that finances the subsidy increases the total indirect tax revenue of the government by Rs 39.84 billion. There is a marginal increase of Rs 0.9 billion in the direct tax revenue and slight declines of Rs 0.76 billion in tariff revenue and Rs 1.31 billion in other revenue. The net increase in overall revenue is Rs 8.99 billion. However, there is no change in the overall government balance.

There is a marginal increase of Rs 0.43 billion in the overall savings of households.

Box 8.1 Poverty effects among agriculture households of a 20 percent increase in world prices of cotton lint and yarn

The 2001–02 SAM that is used to calibrate the CGE model does not differentiate in each of the 19 household groups between households producing cotton and those that do not produce cotton. However, the data from the HIES allow disaggregation of cotton and non-cotton agricultural households in Punjab, Sindh, and other Pakistan. To compute the poverty effects on cotton households of changes in the world price of cotton lint and yarn, we respecify our basic microsimulation to integrate the results on household incomes generated by the CGE model and the cotton/non-cotton distinction in the household survey. Again the calculations are undertaken outside the CGE simulations and are performed for agricultural households only (households h1–h15 in Table 5.4).

Total income of each of the household groups in the CGE is composed of factor incomes (labor, capital, and land) and other incomes (dividends, transfers, and remittances). In this analysis we compare the poverty results on cotton and non-cotton households derived using the CGE results on total income and on factor incomes only. This comparison allows us to separate the effects of the appreciation of the exchange rate on foreign remittances as a result of the increase in world cotton prices from its effects through factor incomes.

The factor incomes are generated in the CGE model on a sectoral basis. The total labor income is the sectoral sum of the product of wages and sectoral employment, both of which are endogenously determined in the model. The total capital income is the sectoral sum of the product of the sectoral return to capital and sectoral capital. The sectoral return to capital is endogenous, while the sectoral capital is fixed. The total land sectoral income (agriculture only) is the sum of the product of the sectoral return to land and sectoral land. The sectoral return to land is endogenous, while the sectoral land is fixed.

To calculate cotton and non-cotton household factor incomes for this analysis, we separate income generated in the cotton sectors from that in the rest of the production sectors. Factor incomes from the cotton sector are derived as the sum of labor income in raw cotton (sector 5) and in cotton lint and yarn (sector 20), capital income in sectors 5 and 20, and land income in sector 5. On the other hand factor incomes for non-cotton households are the sum of labor income, capital income, and land income in all sectors in the model excluding sectors 5 and 20. These factor incomes are distributed among agricultural household groups using the fixed income distribution shares in the SAM.

The accompanying table presents the poverty indexes of cotton and non-cotton agricultural households in Punjab, Sindh, and other Pakistan. Cotton households in Sindh, which account for 10.7 percent of the total agricultural households in Pakistan, have the highest poverty incidence, 53.1 percent. Non-cotton households in the province, which account for 14.9 percent of the agricultural households, have a poverty incidence of 48.4 percent. Punjab province, which accounts for a larger share of agricultural households, has a relatively lower incidence of poverty compared to Sindh. Its cotton households, which account for 14.2 percent of agricultural households, have poverty incidence of 35.3 percent, while its non-cotton households, which account for 25.8 percent of agricultural households, have a poverty incidence of 27.6 percent. There are very few cotton households in other Pakistan, but there are more non-cotton agricultural households. The poverty incidence of cotton households in other Pakistan, 22.6 percent, is lower than the incidence in Sindh and Punjab. The poverty incidence of non-cotton households in other Pakistan, 31.8 percent, is higher than that of non-cotton households in Punjab but lower than that of non-cotton households in Sindh. *(continued)*

Poverty effects among agriculture households

	Sindh		Punjab		Other Pakistan[a]	
	Cotton	Non-cotton	Cotton	Non-cotton	Cotton	Non-cotton
Population distribution (%)[b]	10.7	14.9	14.2	25.8	0.8	33.6
			Index at the base (2001–02)			
Poverty headcount	53.1	48.4	35.3	27.6	22.6	31.8
Poverty gap	12.0	10.8	7.1	5.5	3.6	5.3
Poverty severity	3.9	3.4	2.1	1.6	0.9	1.3
			Percent change from base[c]			
Poverty headcount	–3.8	2.2	–6.4	0.0	–14.3	2.2
Poverty gap	–1.9	3.4	–5.2	0.7	–4.2	4.2
Poverty severity	–1.5	4.2	–6.4	0.9	–5.3	5.6
			Percent change from base[d]			
Poverty headcount	–3.8	1.8	–6.4	0.0	–14.3	2.2
Poverty gap	–2.3	3.2	–5.9	0.3	–5.0	3.9
Poverty severity	–2.1	4.0	–7.3	0.4	–6.3	5.3

[a]Includes only agriculture households (h1–h15). Does not include urban and rural nonfarm households.
[b]Relative to only total agriculture households.
[c]Based on changes in total real household incomes (factor incomes and other household incomes: dividends, transfers, and foreign remittances).
[d]Based on only changes in real factor incomes.

Two sets of poverty results are presented in the table. The first set uses the total household income effect in each group from the CGE simulation involving a 20 percent increase in the world price for cotton lint and yarn, while the second set utilizes only the results for factor incomes. Focusing on the first set, the results indicate that there is poverty reduction in cotton households in all provinces. The highest reduction, 14.3 percent from the base value, is in other Pakistan (which reduces the poverty incidence from 22.6 percent to 19.4 percent). However, this reduction involves few poor households since cotton households in other Pakistan account for only 0.8 percent of all agricultural households. There are more poor cotton households in Punjab, which are favorably affected by the 20 percent increase in the world cotton price. The base poverty incidence in the province declines by 6.4 percent (from a poverty incidence of 35.3 percent to 33 percent). In Sindh the base poverty incidence for cotton households declines by 3.8 percent (from 53.1 percent to 51 percent). Non-cotton households in Sindh and other Pakistan suffer from increasing poverty when cotton prices increase.

The second set of poverty effects involves changes in only factor incomes. The source of the difference is the income loss in foreign remittances as a result of the 1.88 percent appreciation in the exchange rate (Table 8.6), which affects household incomes. Foreign remittances account for 5.3 percent of all the household incomes (Table 5.5), a simplification in the SAM. Under this specification the loss in income from remittances does not noticeably affect the incidence of poverty but affects the poverty gap and poverty severity for cotton households in all provinces. There is more of a reduction in these two indexes if remittance income is not taken into account. For non-cotton households in Sindh province, the increase in three poverty indexes is relatively smaller compared to the results in which findings on total household income are utilized. For non-cotton households in Punjab and other Pakistan, there is no difference in the poverty incidence, but there is slightly less of an increase in the poverty gap and poverty severity in the case where factors incomes are used.

Using partial equilibrium analysis, Orden et al. (2008) conducted several world cotton price scenario simulations and analyzed their impact on poverty among cotton-producing households in Pakistan. In the case of a 20 percent increase in the world price of cotton, their results indicate that the poverty headcount index in Sindh declines by 36 percent and that in Punjab by 25 percent from the respective poverty index baseline values. Although the results presented in the box also show declining poverty indexes in both provinces as a result of a 20 percent increase in the world price of cotton, the magnitudes of the declines are much lower. The difference lies in the method used to measure the impact of the cotton price increase on the incomes of cotton-producing households.

In the study by Orden et al. (2008), a 20 percent increase in domestic cotton prices is assumed to translate, for a fixed quantity supplied, into an equal percentage increase of gross cotton revenue of cotton-producing households, with net cotton income (gross revenue minus production expenses) from sales at the higher price increasing more in percentage terms than the price. Other output and factor prices and the other income of cotton households are assumed to be constant. In contrast the CGE results consider a 20 percent increase in world prices for cotton lint, which implies less of an increase of domestic prices for cotton lint and yarn and raw cotton.

Moreover, in the CGE model the impacts on the incomes of cotton-producing households, as well as on the rest of the economy, are determined through the effects on factor prices and factor demands. In Table 8.8 the 20 percent increase in the world price of cotton results in the real wage of unskilled farm labor improving by 13.25 percent and in average real returns to land increasing by 7.68 percent. Returns to capital and land used in cotton production increase by over 27 percent (Table 8.7). However, because there is a decline in the output price of textiles and other industries (excluding lint and yarn) and the entire service sector (Table 8.7), real returns to factors that are used heavily in other sectors decline. Thus real wages of skilled labor decline by 0.45 percent, those of unskilled workers by 0.26 percent, and average returns to capital by 0.80 percent. Cotton-producing households also rely on these factors as an income source. Thus the effects on the net incomes of cotton-producing households from the assumed 20 percent increase in world cotton prices in the CGE model are less than the income effects derived under the assumptions of the partial equilibrium analysis.

A second difference between the partial equilibrium and CGE analyses is that the incomes of non-cotton-producing households are assumed constant in the partial equilibrium analysis, so poverty is not affected among these households. In the CGE analysis incomes of these other households are affected by the change in world cotton prices, with poverty falling among all rural households but rising among urban households. Overall the CGE analysis implies less of a reduction of poverty in Pakistan from a 20 percent increase in the world price of cotton than is implied by the partial equilibrium analysis of such an increase.

Table 8.11 Intersectoral effects: SIM 3, increase in production subsidy (percent change from base)

Commodities	Output		Domestic demand			Exports		Imports		Returns to:	
	Output	Output price	Domestic demand	Domestic price (including indirect tax)	Investment	Exports	Export price in local currency	Imports	Import price in local currency	Capital	Land
SIM 3a: 5% increase in production subsidy to the textile sector											
Raw cotton	–1.48	–3.17	–1.48	–3.17	–11.31	—	—	—	—	–5.34	–5.34
Cotton lint and yarn	–1.65	–1.55	2.41	–1.39	–10.38	–12.61	–2.01	20.02	–2.02	–4.84	—
Textiles	5.67	2.97	2.77	–2.28	45.04	10.07	–2.01	–4.04	–2.01	21.05	—
Agriculture	–0.18	–1.68	–0.18	–1.67	–4.48	–0.52	–2.01	0.12	–2.01	–1.77	–4.08
Excluding raw cotton	–0.11	–1.59	–0.10	–1.58	–4.41	–0.52	–2.01	0.12	–2.01	–1.73	–3.93
Industry	0.60	0.14	0.41	–0.67	4.00	1.36	–2.01	0.45	–2.01	2.11	—
Excluding cotton lint and yarn, and textiles	–0.63	–0.50	–0.30	–0.26	–3.11	–2.69	–2.01	0.38	–2.01	–1.14	—
Services	–0.14	0.32	–0.09	0.42	–0.96	–1.12	–2.01	2.73	–2.01	0.03	—
Total	0.14	–0.15	0.06	–0.41	–0.17	0.85	–2.01	0.56	–2.01	0.29	–4.08
SIM 3b: 5% increase in production subsidy to the cotton lint and yarn sector											
Raw cotton	4.07	3.98	4.07	3.99	18.19	—	—	—	—	8.43	8.43
Cotton lint and yarn	4.60	4.06	1.25	–1.28	41.66	13.58	–0.82	–9.73	–0.82	18.71	—
Textiles	–0.74	–0.79	–0.25	–0.77	–4.29	–1.49	–0.82	1.00	–0.82	–2.42	—
Agriculture	0.07	0.50	0.11	0.53	–0.71	–1.79	–0.82	0.94	–0.82	–0.62	1.67
Excluding raw cotton	–0.16	0.30	–0.13	0.32	–0.91	–1.79	–0.82	0.94	–0.82	–0.72	0.85
Industry	0.07	0.03	–0.03	–0.31	1.21	0.48	–0.82	0.11	–0.82	0.21	—
Excluding cotton lint and yarn, and textiles	–0.24	–0.21	–0.12	–0.12	–1.17	–0.97	–0.82	0.17	–0.82	–0.85	—

Services	–0.05	–0.27	–0.04	–0.25	–0.48	–0.30	–0.82	0.74	–0.82	–0.50	—
Total	0.02	0.00	–0.01	–0.10	0.00	0.25	–0.82	0.17	–0.82	–0.30	1.67
SIM 3c: 5% increase in production subsidy to the raw cotton sector											
Raw cotton	1.20	1.17	1.20	–3.89	5.14	—	—	—	—	2.46	2.46
Cotton lint and yarn	1.36	–0.35	0.38	–0.39	11.03	3.97	–0.25	–3.09	–0.25	5.28	—
Textiles	–0.22	–0.24	–0.07	–0.23	–1.29	–0.44	–0.25	0.29	–0.25	–0.73	—
Agriculture	0.02	0.14	0.04	–0.14	–0.09	–0.53	–0.25	0.28	–0.25	–0.13	0.49
Excluding raw cotton	–0.04	0.08	–0.03	0.08	–0.14	–0.53	–0.25	0.28	–0.25	–0.15	0.25
Industry	0.02	–0.13	–0.01	–0.10	0.26	0.14	–0.25	0.03	–0.24	0.04	—
Excluding cotton lint and yarn, and textiles	–0.07	–0.07	–0.03	–0.04	–0.35	–0.29	–0.25	0.05	–0.24	–0.26	—
Services	–0.02	–0.08	–0.01	–0.08	–0.14	–0.09	–0.25	0.22	–0.25	–0.15	—
Total	0.01	–0.06	0.00	–0.10	–0.00	0.07	–0.25	0.05	–0.24	–0.08	0.49
SIM 3d: 5% increase in production subsidy to the textile sector[a]											
Raw cotton	–1.41	–3.51	–1.41	–3.51	–10.55	—	—	—	—	–5.13	–5.13
Cotton lint and yarn	–1.57	–2.27	2.54	–2.12	–8.95	–12.67	–2.73	20.39	–2.74	–4.29	—
Textiles	5.83	2.21	2.88	–3.01	47.92	10.31	–2.73	–4.05	–2.73	22.00	—
Agriculture	–0.19	–2.04	–0.18	–2.03	–4.10	–0.88	–2.73	0.33	–2.74	–1.77	–4.05
Excluding raw cotton	–0.12	–1.95	–0.11	–1.94	–4.03	–0.88	–2.73	0.33	–2.74	–1.74	–3.92
Industry	0.67	–0.52	0.47	–1.30	5.18	1.43	–2.73	0.44	–2.73	2.46	—
Excluding cotton lint and yarn, and textiles	–0.59	–1.12	–0.25	–0.86	–2.30	–2.72	–2.73	0.36	–2.73	–0.94	—
Services	–0.15	–0.27	–0.10	–0.16	–1.76	–1.27	–2.73	3.01	–2.73	–0.59	—
Total	0.16	–0.72	0.07	–0.96	–0.08	0.87	–2.73	0.57	–2.73	0.11	–4.05

Note: Using compensatory consumption tax.
[a]Using compensatory income tax.

However, it is not enough to offset the drop in foreign savings valued in rupees. Thus the overall nominal savings of the economy decline. The 0.39 percent decline in the price of investment is not enough to offset the drop in overall nominal savings. Therefore overall real investment drops by 0.17 percent.

Because of the appreciation of the exchange rate with a textile production subsidy, exports of cotton lint and yarn drop by 12.61 percent (Table 8.11). The 2.41 percent increase in domestic demand is not enough to offset the drop in exports. Thus overall output of cotton lint and yarn drops by 1.65 percent. This in turn results in output of raw

Table 8.12 Macro effects: SIM 3, increase in production subsidy

	SIM 3a	SIM 3b	SIM 3c	SIM 3d[a]
		Change from base (%)		
Real consumption	0.23	0.02	0.02	0.26
Real investment	–0.17	0.00	–0.00	–0.08
Real exports	0.85	0.25	0.07	0.87
Real import	0.56	0.17	0.05	0.57
Real exchange rate	–2.01	–0.82	–0.25	–2.73
Export prices	–2.01	–0.82	–0.25	–2.73
Import prices	–2.01	–0.82	–0.24	–2.73
Household consumer price index[b]	–0.06	–0.03	–0.02	–1.25
Composite price	–0.07	–0.01	–0.06	–1.22
Domestic price	–0.41	–0.10	–0.10	–0.96
Price of investment	–0.39	–0.32	–0.10	–1.62
		Amount (billion Rs)		
Government balance	0.00	0.00	0.00	0.00
Total government income	8.99	0.92	0.24	5.96
Tariff revenue	–0.76	–0.20	–0.06	–1.12
Indirect tax revenue	39.84	13.13	4.13	–3.74
Direct tax revenue	0.90	–0.33	–0.10	41.62
Other revenue	–1.31	0.54	0.16	–1.30
Subsidy	–29.67	–12.21	–3.88	–29.50
Total household savings	0.43	–0.34	–0.11	–4.49
Foreign savings	–3.37	–1.37	–0.42	–4.57
Firm savings	0.00	0.00	0.00	0.00
Overall savings[c]	–2.93	–1.71	–0.52	–9.06

Notes: Using compensatory consumption tax. SIM 3a, 5 percent increase in production subsidy to the textiles sector; SIM 3b, 5 percent increase in production subsidy to the cotton lint and yarn sector; SIM 3c, 5 percent increase in production subsidy to the raw cotton sector; SIM 3d, 5 percent increase in production subsidy to the textile sector.

[a]Using compensatory direct income tax.

[b]Composite price weighted by consumption expenditure.

[c]Sum of government balance, total household savings, foreign savings, and firm savings.

Table 8.13 Factor price effects: SIM 3, increase in production subsidy (percent change from base)

	SIM 3a		SIM 3b		SIM 3c		SIM 3d[a]	
Factor prices	Real[b]	Nominal	Real	Nominal	Real	Nominal	Real	Nominal
Skilled labor	1.81	1.75	0.06	0.03	0.01	–0.01	3.31	2.06
Unskilled farm labor	–4.06	–4.12	3.59	3.56	1.05	1.03	–2.76	–4.01
Unskilled workers	–0.09	–0.15	–0.23	–0.26	–0.06	–0.08	1.28	0.03
Average returns to capital	0.35	0.29	–0.27	–0.30	–0.06	–0.08	1.36	0.11
Average returns to land	–4.02	–4.08	1.70	1.67	0.51	0.49	–2.80	–4.05

Notes: Using compensatory consumption tax. SIM 3a, 5 percent increase in production subsidy to the textiles sector; SIM 3b, 5 percent increase in production subsidy to the cotton lint and yarn sector; SIM 3c, 5 percent increase in production subsidy to the raw cotton sector; SIM 3d, 5 percent increase in production subsidy to the textile sector.

[a]Using compensatory direct income tax.

[b]Less change in consumer price index.

cotton that is 1.48 percent lower. Increased imports of cotton lint and yarn, together with higher domestic demand, provide the input requirements for higher output in the textile sector.

Table 8.13 indicates that, since raw cotton is negatively affected, the impact on the wages of farm labor and the average returns to land are negative as well. The effect on the wages of unskilled workers is also negative, but there are increases in the wages of skilled labor and returns to capital, both of which are used intensively in textile production.

Overall household income in real terms declines by 0.05 percent. The income of all urban households improves by 0.58 percent (Table 8.14). However, within urban households the income of the urban poor declines by 0.14 percent. Therefore the improvement in the income of urban households comes at the expense of the income of rural households (which declines by 0.71 percent) and poor urban households. As a result, a production subsidy to the textile sector raises poverty levels. All poverty indexes under SIM 3a indicate increased poverty, especially in the rural areas (Table 8.15).

The results under SIM 3b, which involves a production subsidy to the cotton lint and yarn sector, can be interpreted in the same way. Its output price increases by 4.06 percent, while its domestic price declines by 1.28 percent (Table 8.11). Its output improves by 4.6 percent. Its exports improve by 13.58 percent because there is a greater decline in domestic price (1.28 percent) relative to the drop in export price (0.82 percent). Since the share of exports of cotton lint and yarn in overall exports is smaller (about 12 percent) than their share in textile exports, the impact on the appreciation of the real exchange rate is significantly lower. The exchange rate appreciates by only 0.82 percent. The increase in cotton lint and yarn exports is enough to offset the drop in exports of the rest of the sectors. Thus overall exports of the economy improve by 0.25 percent (Table 8.12).

At Rs 12.21 billion, the amount of the subsidy to the cotton lint and yarn sector is significantly lower than that to the textile sector. The increase in the consumption tax is also lower: the increase in indirect tax revenue is only Rs 13.13 billion. Foreign savings in rupees also decline, and so do household savings. Thus overall nominal savings drop. However, the decline in the price of investment is just enough to off-

Table 8.14 Real income effects: SIM 3, increase in production subsidy (percent)

	Population distribution	Real income change from base			
		SIM 3a	SIM 3b	SIM 3c	SIM 3d[a]
Pakistan	—	–0.05	–0.01	–0.0013	–0.08
Urban	28.6	0.58	–0.17	–0.05	–0.48
Urban poor	8.1	–0.14	–0.33	–0.09	1.09
Rural	71.4	–0.71	0.16	0.05	0.33
Farmers[b]	34.2	–1.22	0.49	0.15	–0.21
Workers[c]	6.6	0.00	–0.37	–0.10	1.06
Other rural households[d]	30.7	0.05	–0.31	–0.09	1.13
Other rural poor households	16.8	0.08	–0.37	–0.10	1.09

Notes: Using compensatory consumption tax. SIM 3a, 5 percent increase in production subsidy to the textiles sector; SIM 3b, 5 percent increase in production subsidy to the cotton lint and yarn sector; SIM 3c, 5 percent increase in production subsidy to the raw cotton sector; SIM 3d, 5 percent increase in production subsidy to the textiles sector. See Table 5.4 for definitions of the household groups.
[a]Using compensatory direct income tax.
[b]Large, medium, small, and landless in Punjab, Sindh, and other Pakistan.
[c]Landless agricultural workers in Punjab, Sindh, and other Pakistan.
[d]Nonfarm rural households.

set the drop in nominal savings (investment). Thus overall real investment does not change.

The improvement in output of cotton lint and yarn translates to higher output and price for raw cotton (Table 8.11). These improve the wages of farm labor and the average returns to land shown in Table 8.13. The decline in the average returns to capital and the wages of unskilled workers can be attributed to the slight decline in the output of the textile sector.

Overall real household income drops marginally by 0.01 percent. The drop in the output of the textile sector translates to lower income for urban non-poor households, which declines by 0.17 percent. The drop in the income of the urban poor is due largely to the lower wages of unskilled workers (this group relies on unskilled labor for 76.2 percent of its overall household income; Table 5.5) and to a lesser extent to lower average returns to capital (18 percent of its income comes from capital). Both of these factors are also responsible for the drop in the income of rural non-farmers. However, rural farmers will benefit because of the positive effect on raw cotton. Poverty increases under SIM 3b. However, there is a very slight decline in the rural poverty headcount index due to the increase in income of rural farmers.

The subsidy to the raw cotton sector under SIM 3c is Rs 3.88 billion, which is significantly smaller than the subsidies in SIM 3a and SIM 3b. Its impacts are relatively smaller as well. It yields slightly favorable effects on the sector in terms of output and factor prices. There is zero change in the overall real income of households. However, there are differential effects across household groups. Urban households and rural non-farmers are worse off, while farmers are better off. Poverty increases in both urban and rural areas.

SIM 3d calls for the same subsidy to the textile sector, but this time it is financed by a compensatory tax on income. Although the same 5 percent subsidy is applied to the textile sector, the sectoral effects (Table 8.11) are not all the same as in SIM 3a. This is because the compensatory consump-

Table 8.15 Poverty effects: SIM 3, increase in production subsidy (percent change from base)

Poverty index	Pakistan	Urban	Rural
		SIM 3a	
Poverty headcount	1.05	0.00	1.39
Poverty gap	1.58	0.59	1.87
Poverty severity	1.76	0.69	2.07
		SIM 3b	
Poverty headcount	0.09	0.47	–0.03
Poverty gap	0.72	1.35	0.53
Poverty severity	0.95	1.58	0.77
		SIM 3c	
Poverty headcount	0.11	0.19	0.09
Poverty gap	0.19	0.38	0.13
Poverty severity	0.24	0.45	0.19
		SIM 3d[a]	
Poverty headcount	–2.45	–1.71	–2.68
Poverty gap	–3.58	–4.34	–3.36
Poverty severity	–4.34	–5.08	–4.13

Notes: Using compensatory consumption tax. SIM 3a, 5 percent increase in production subsidy to the textile sector; SIM 3b, 5 percent increase in production subsidy to the cotton lint and yarn sector; SIM 3c, 5 percent increase in production subsidy to the raw cotton sector; SIM 3d, 5 percent increase in production subsidy to the textile sector.
[a]Using compensatory direct income tax.

tion tax under SIM 3a affects the sectoral relative prices, whereas the compensatory income tax under the present case does not. The textile sector is favorably affected, as indicated by its higher output and prices. Raw cotton and cotton lint and yarn experience lower output and output price. A relative price change leads to higher textile exports compared with domestic demand. Since the textile sector has a large export share, overall exports expand by 0.87 percent (Table 8.12). However, the rest of the sectors experience declining exports because of the 2.73 percent appreciation of the real exchange rate. Overall imports increase by 0.57 percent because of the appreciation of the exchange rate.

The amount of the subsidy is Rs 29.50 billion, which is marginally lower than that in SIM 3a. The slight difference is due to the different sectoral results. The revenue from direct income tax increases by Rs 41.62 billion because of the compensatory income tax. Total household savings decline by Rs 4.49 billion and foreign savings by Rs 4.57 billion. Thus overall savings decline. However, the 0.08 percent decline in real investment is smaller than that in SIM 3a. This is because the 1.62 percent decline in the price of investment is higher than in SIM 3a.

There is an increase in the real wages of skilled labor and unskilled workers and in the average return to capital (Table 8.13). However, the wages of unskilled farm labor and the average return to land drop. Overall income declines by 0.08 percent (Table 8.14). The income of urban households declines by 0.48 percent, largely due to the drop in the income of urban non-poor households, because the burden of the additional income tax levied to finance the subsidy falls on them. Urban poor households, however, experience higher income. The income of farmers decreases by 0.21 percent. This drop is smaller than the decline under SIM 3a.

There is a notable reduction in poverty. This is because consumers benefit from the 1.21 percent reduction in the consumer price (Table 8.12) and from the income transfer from the urban non-poor to the rest of the household groups through the compensatory income tax.

CHAPTER 9

Dynamic Analysis of an Increase in Total Factor Productivity

Recent developments in the world market for cotton and textiles present challenges for Pakistan. One such development was the abolition of the MFA in 2005. In the international market without the MFA quotas, world demand becomes more price responsive. Thus competitive, low-cost suppliers could gain market share. This scenario presents opportunities for Pakistan if it enhances the competitiveness of the cotton-textile sectors through productivity improvement. One key sector is raw cotton. After Bt cotton technology was introduced in 2002, India's production of cotton surged (Table 2.2). Although there are ongoing efforts in Pakistan to develop Bt cotton technology, the country has not yet formally implemented a Bt cotton program, and its relative competitiveness will suffer.

As discussed in Chapter 3, another major challenge facing the sector is how to improve the quality of cotton. Its poor quality is the result of contamination as it passes through the various stages of the production and marketing chain and is also due the use of old machinery and primitive saw gins. Altaf (2008) notes that while the international standard for ginning productivity has reached 60 bales per hour, Pakistan is only operating at 10–12 bales per hour.

Upgrading the present technology is therefore one of the major challenges for the ginning sector. Increasing the efficiency of farm and trading management is also necessary. Standardization to reduce contamination is critical. But there are institutional bottlenecks. The Cotton Standardization Ordinance, which was passed in 2002, failed to generate significant improvement because the textile industry has not been willing to pay an adequate premium for higher-quality cotton. This resistance has held back progress to a large extent (Salam 2008), suggesting a need to search for lower-cost methods to improve quality.

The spinning sector in Pakistan produces yarn that is of lower count and thus commands relatively low prices in the international market. The weaving sector is too dependent on cotton fibers, and Pakistan produces fewer blends than its competitors. Although the production shares of blended cloth and dyed and printed cloth have improved lately, Pakistan still concentrates on the production of gray cloth, which is unprocessed and so commands low prices in the world market.

All of this indicates significant room for productivity improvement in the cotton-textile value chain in Pakistan. A detailed assessment of specific industry strategies and an analysis of how they might affect productivity is outside the scope of this report. Instead our analysis focuses on the intersectoral and income implications for Pakistan of enhanced international competitiveness in the cotton-textile sectors, by assessing the effects of exogenous assumed improvements in TFP. Since improved TFP has long-term implications, we extend our CGE model into a dynamic-recursive form to capture the economywide effects over time.

Figure 9.1 Change in output: SIM 4a

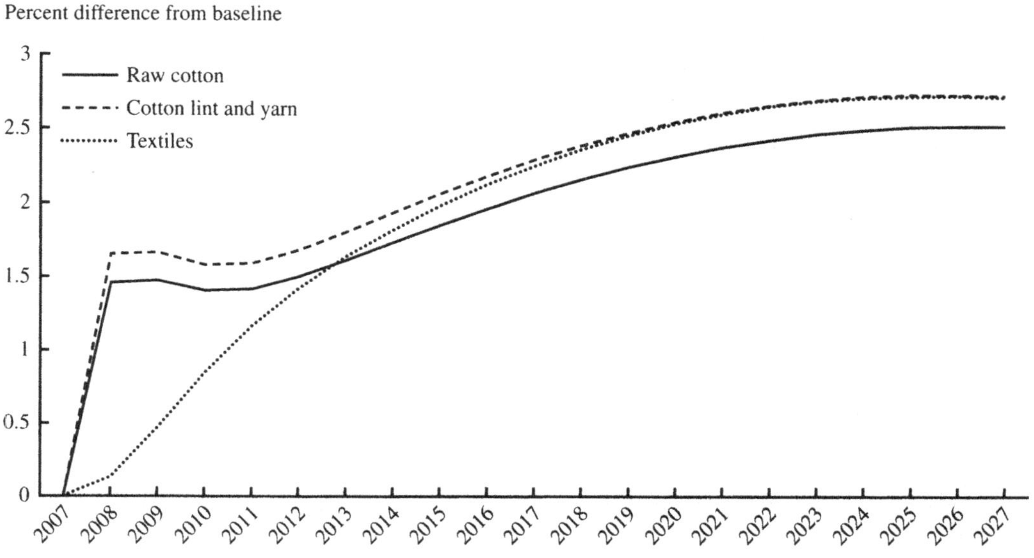

Note: SIM 4a: 5 percent TFP increase in raw cotton.

Specifically we generate a baseline scenario without TFP improvement from 2001 to 2027, assuming an increase of the labor supply of 2 percent per year based on the historical population trend in Pakistan.[1] Sectoral capital stock is updated annually using a capital accumulation equation. The supply of land is fixed, but land use varies across agricultural sectors. In this analysis we take 2008 as the first year in which a permanent improvement in productivity occurs. We evaluate three scenarios: increasing by 5 percent the TFP for raw cotton production only, increasing the TFP of the raw cotton and cotton lint and yarn sectors simultaneously, and also increasing the TFP in textiles. For each scenario we take the percent difference from the dynamic simulation results with and without TFP improvement and analyze the economywide and household income effects.

In the analysis that follows, percent change (increase or decrease) means percent difference of the variables from the baseline values. We present the results for key variables in graphical form over the 20-year time period. We do not attempt to project forward disaggregated household data, hence in this analysis we do not undertake microsimulation-based analysis of effects on poverty among different types of households.

TFP Improvement in Raw Cotton

An improvement in TFP in the raw cotton sector alone increases production (Figure 9.1) and drives down its domestic price (Figure 9.2). The decline in its domestic price exceeds the increase in production because raw cotton is not exported but is instead a raw material used in cotton lint and yarn production. The raw cotton sector sells 89 percent of its output to the cotton lint and yarn sector. The effects of the productivity improvement in raw cotton are therefore limited by the absorptive capacity of the cotton lint and yarn sector, which operates along its old production function because

[1]As described in note 2 in Chapter 7, recent annual population growth has been 1.9 percent.

Figure 9.2 Change in output price: SIM 4a

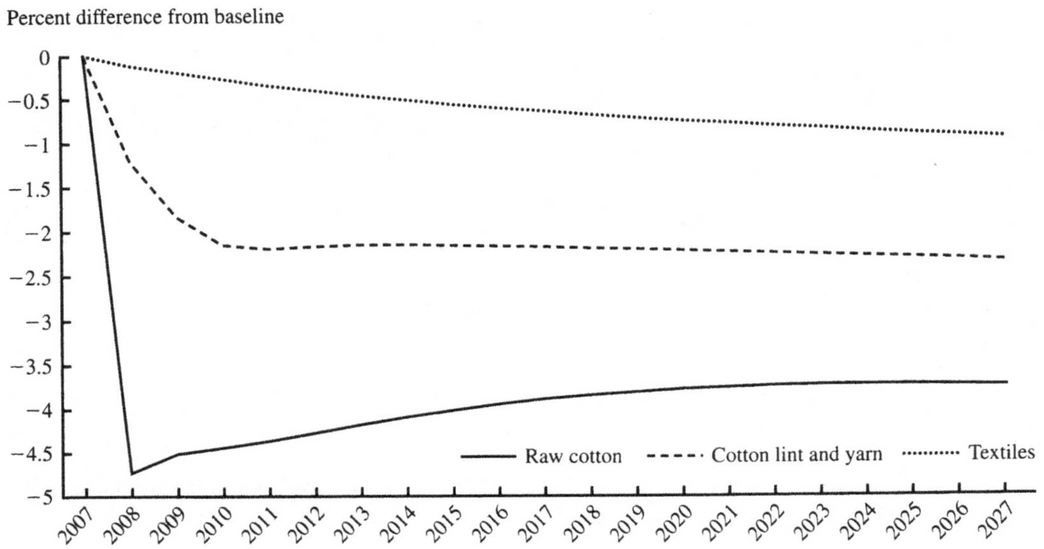

Note: SIM 4a: 5 percent TFP increase in raw cotton.

there is no corresponding increase in its TFP. The improved productivity in raw cotton immediately benefits the cotton lint and yarn sector (Figure 9.1). Output of cotton lint and yarn increases relative to the baseline and its exports expand (Figure 9.3). There is capital inflow into the sector because of relatively higher returns (Figure 9.4).

There is a lagged response in the domestic textile sector. Initially the output effect is positive but minimal in 2008 (Figure 9.1), as the industry competes with the export of cotton lint and yarn for its inputs. Then, as capital accumulates in the textile sector because of increasing return to capital (Figure 9.4), its output improves and converges after about four years toward the increase in raw cotton and cotton lint and yarn production over the baseline (Figure 9.1).

There is an increase in real income over time from a TFP improvement in raw cotton (Figure 9.5). Differential effects across household groups are largely due to the dynamic interaction effects across the cotton-related sectors and the rest of the economy. Farmers' wages and returns to land (Figure 9.6) initially decline relative to the baseline values. The incomes of large and medium farmers, small farmers, and agricultural workers initially fall. The incomes of large and medium farmers drop further from the baseline than the incomes of small farmers and agricultural workers. However, as the other sectors adjust over time, factor prices improve, leading to higher income for all households.

TFP Improvement in Raw Cotton and Cotton Lint and Yarn

An improvement in TFP in both raw cotton and cotton lint and yarn initially increases the output of both sectors relative to the baseline (Figure 9.7), with prices for the output of both sectors declining (Figure 9.8). The increase in output in 2008 is higher than in the previous scenario because the absorptive capacity of the cotton lint and yarn sector improves with its increased TFP. With lower raw cotton input costs, and the reduction in the cost of producing cotton lint and yarn resulting from its improved TFP, the export competitiveness of the sector initially surges relative to the baseline (Figure 9.9).

Figure 9.3 Change in exports: SIM 4a

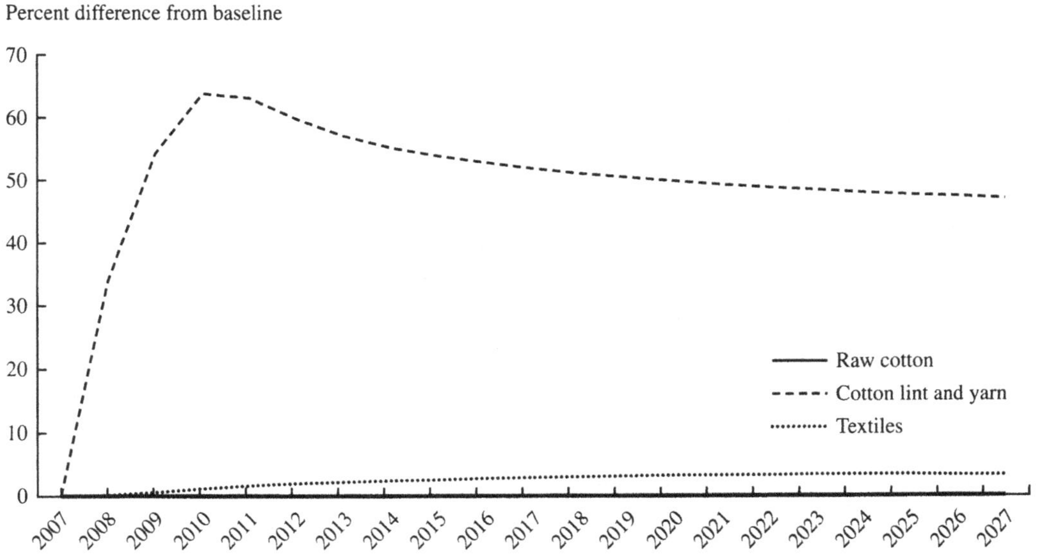

Note: SIM 4a: 5 percent TFP increase in raw cotton.

Figure 9.4 Change in returns to capital: SIM 4a

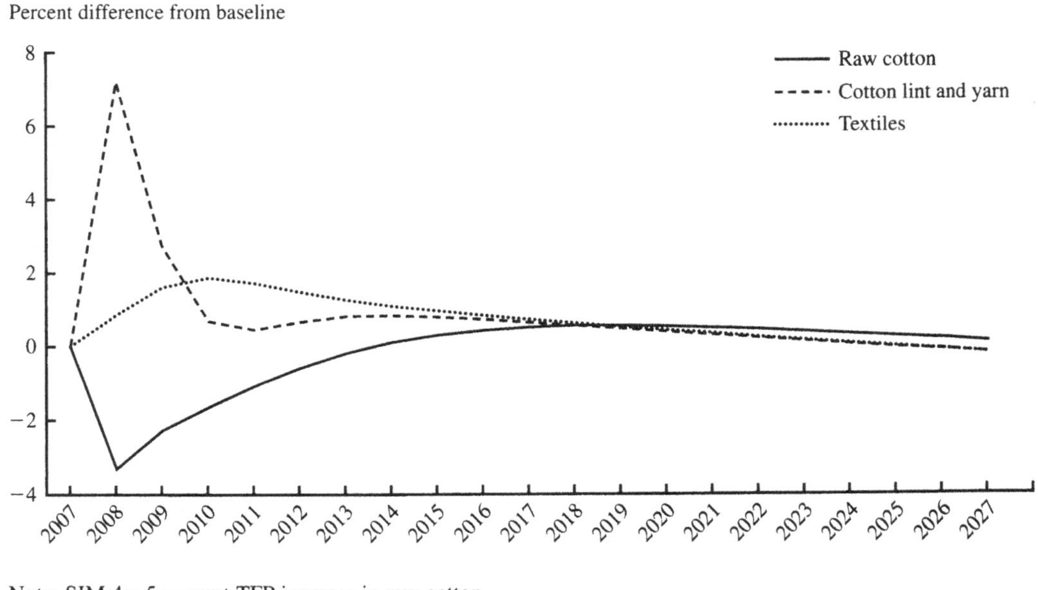

Note: SIM 4a: 5 percent TFP increase in raw cotton.

Figure 9.5 Change in real income: SIM 4a

Percent difference from baseline

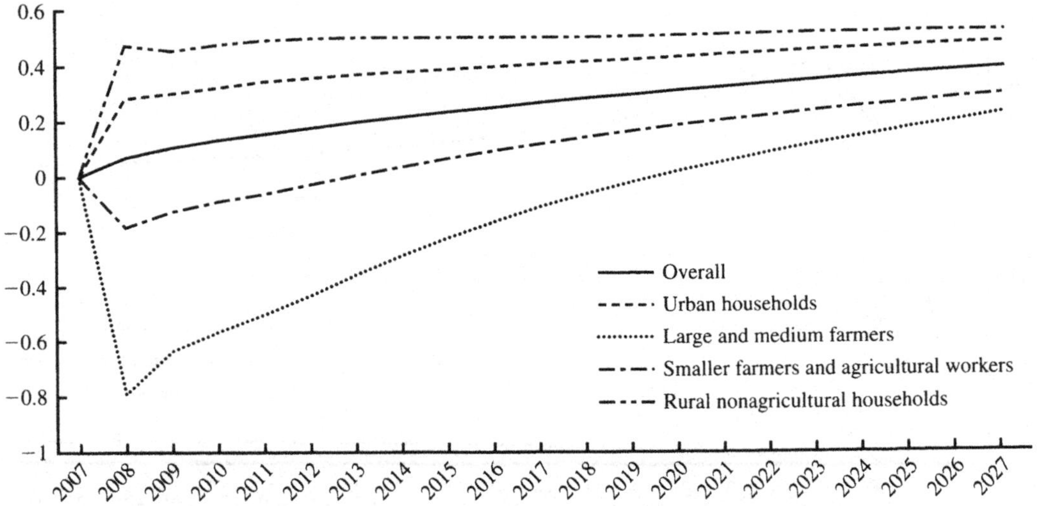

Note: SIM 4a: 5 percent TFP increase in raw cotton.

Figure 9.6 Change in wages and return to land: SIM 4a

Percent difference from baseline

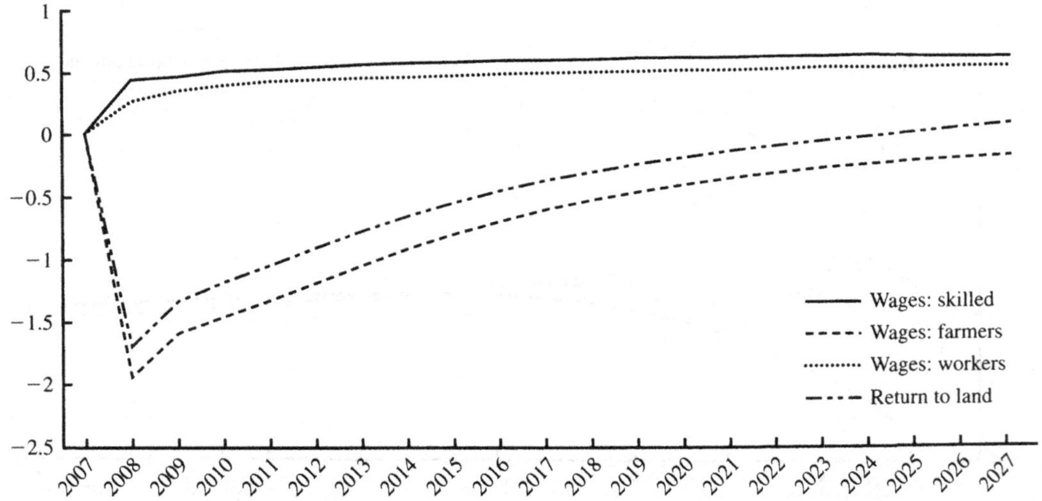

Note: SIM 4a: 5 percent TFP increase in raw cotton.

Figure 9.7 Change in output: SIM 4b

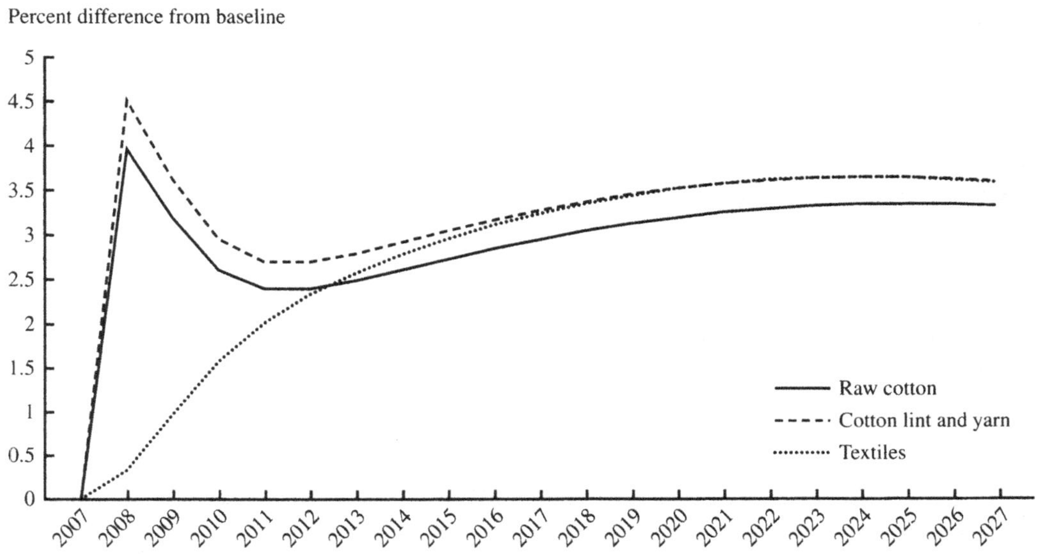

Note: SIM 4b: 5 percent TFP increase in raw cotton and cotton lint and yarn.

Figure 9.8 Change in output price: SIM 4b

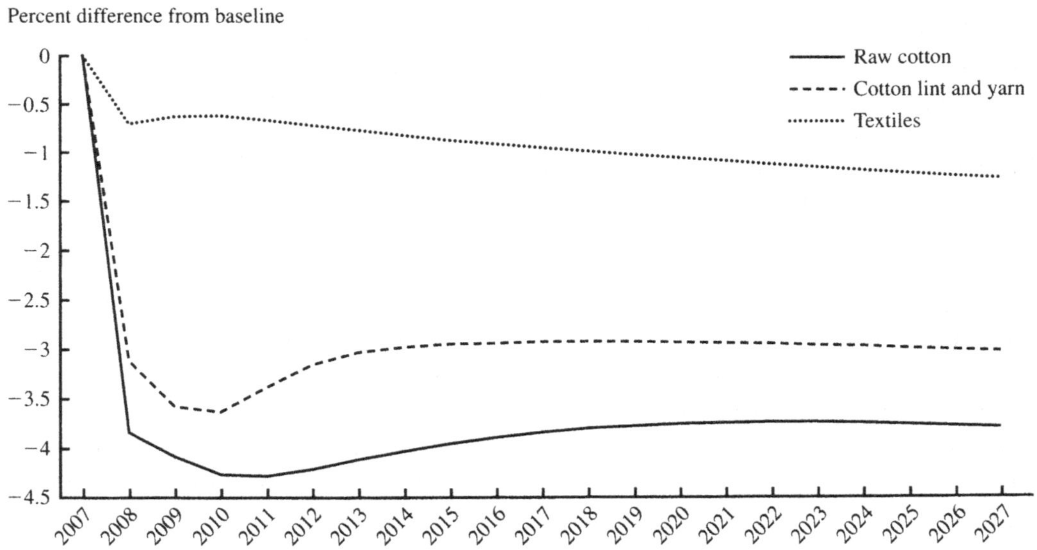

Note: SIM 4b: 5 percent TFP increase in raw cotton and cotton lint and yarn.

Figure 9.9 Change in exports: SIM 4b

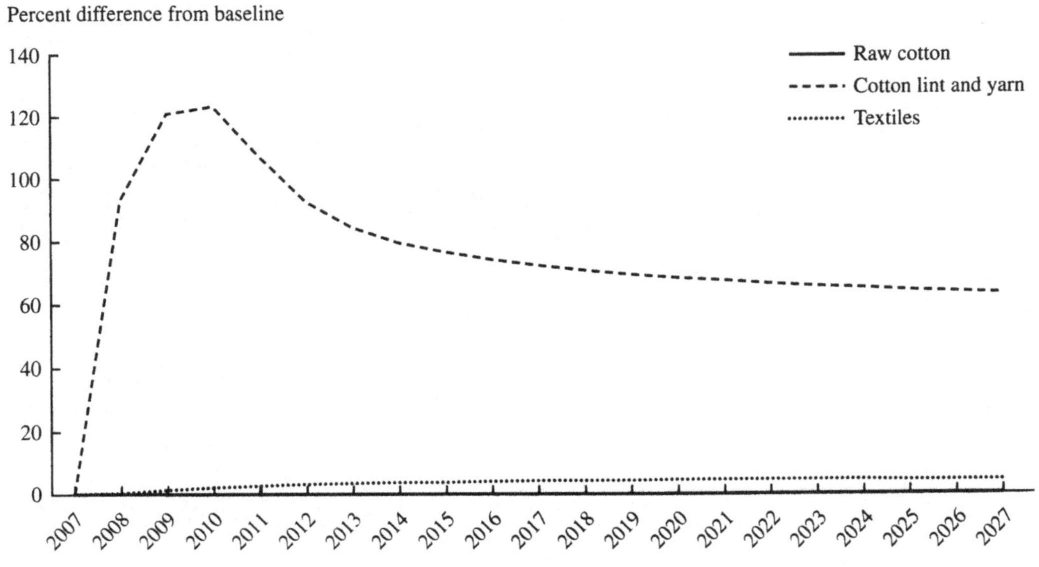

Note: SIM 4b: 5 percent TFP increase in raw cotton and cotton lint and yarn.

Again, the initial effects on the textile sector are positive but minimal. This is because the increased output of cotton lint and yarn goes to the export market. In 2009 the improvement in exports of cotton lint and yarn starts to taper off. Some of the improvement in the output of cotton lint and yarn flows to the domestic local textile sector at lower cost. Furthermore the rate of return to capital in the textile sector continues to increase (Figure 9.10) and attracts capital. A period of dynamic adjustment occurs through 2012, then over the long run output converges across the three sectors to a level about 3.5 percent higher than the baseline.

With the TFP of raw cotton and cotton lint and yarn increased, the level of output of raw cotton rises more than in the previous scenario, and the income of small farmers and agricultural workers increases above the baseline in the initial years (Figure 9.11). Large and medium farmers suffer less initial decline in real income, and there is a shorter adjustment to higher income levels than in the baseline for these farmers.

In the previous scenario, farm wages drop by about 2 percent in 2008 (Figure 9.6), whereas in the present scenario they decline by only about 0.5 percent (Figure 9.12). The increase in the wages of workers is similar in both scenarios. In the previous scenario, the rate of return to land declines by 2 percent in 2008, whereas in the present scenario it declines by only about 0.5 percent. The decline in the rate of return to capital in cotton lint and yarn is about 2 percent in 2008 (Figure 9.10), whereas in the previous scenario it was an increase of about 7 percent (Figure 9.4). Farm wages and returns to land continue to decline in 2009 and 2010 in the present scenario, but the decline compared with the baseline is less than that in the previous scenario.

TFP Improvement in Raw Cotton, Cotton Lint and Yarn, and Textiles

The third analysis involves a 5 percent increase in TFP in all three cotton-related sectors. The output effects are presented in Figure 9.13. In 2008 the effect on the output of raw cotton and cotton lint and yarn is similar to that in the second scenario, but the effect on the output of textiles is sig-

Figure 9.10 Change in returns to capital: SIM 4b

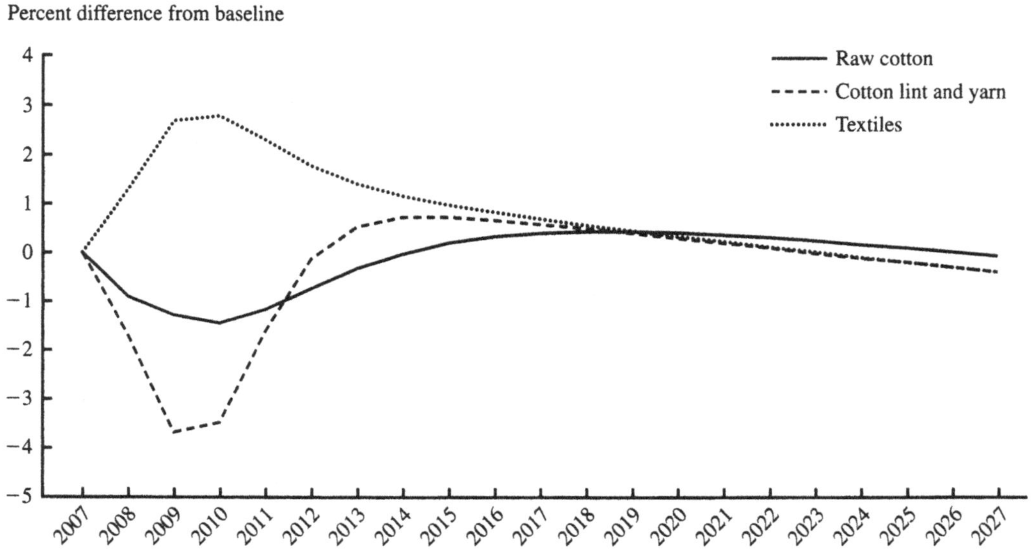

Note: SIM 4b: 5 percent TFP increase in raw cotton and cotton lint and yarn.

Figure 9.11 Change in real income: SIM 4b

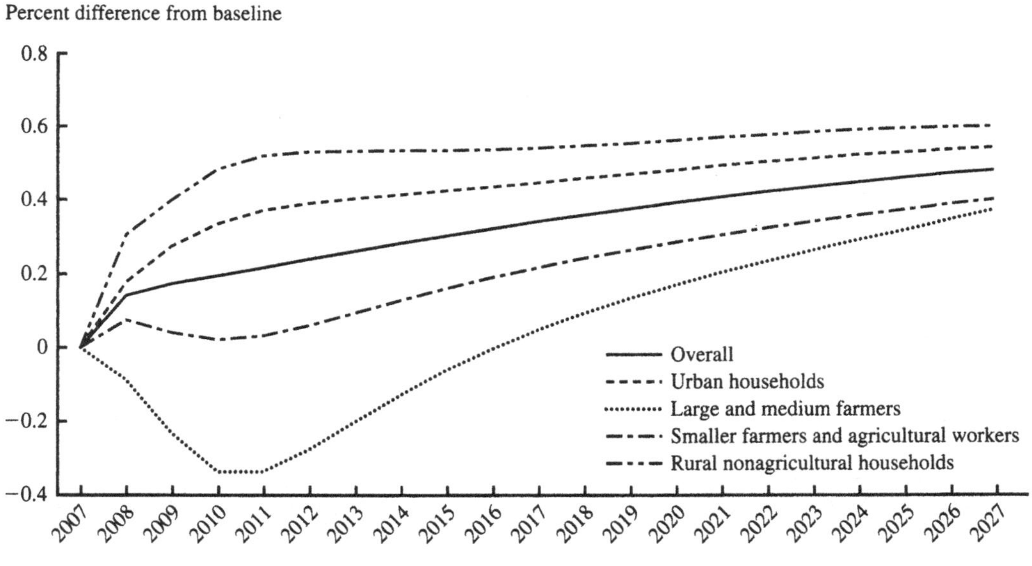

Note: SIM 4b: 5 percent TFP increase in raw cotton and cotton lint and yarn.

Figure 9.12 Change in wages and return to land: SIM 4b

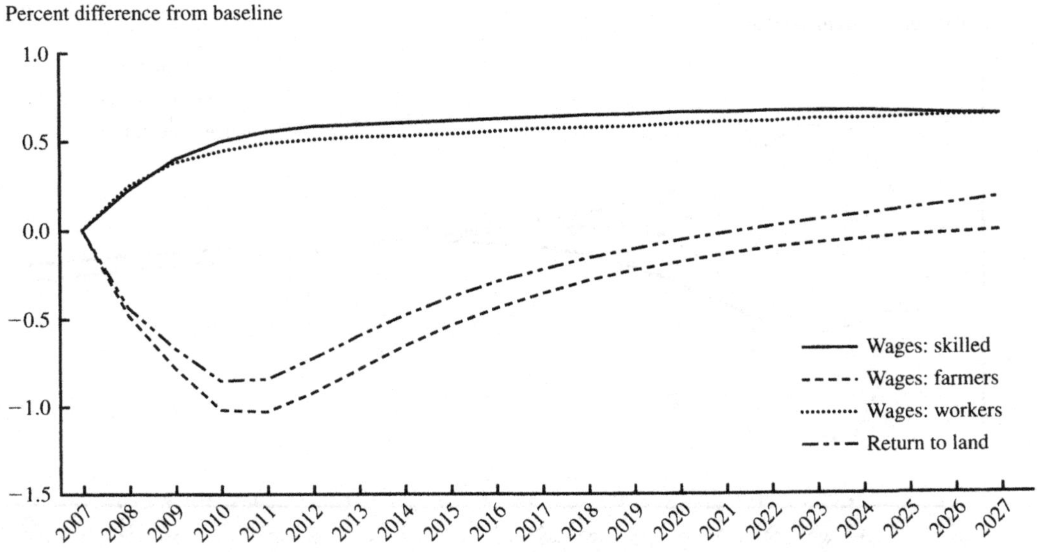

Note: SIM 4b: 5 percent TFP increase in raw cotton and cotton lint and yarn.

Figure 9.13 Change in output: SIM 4c

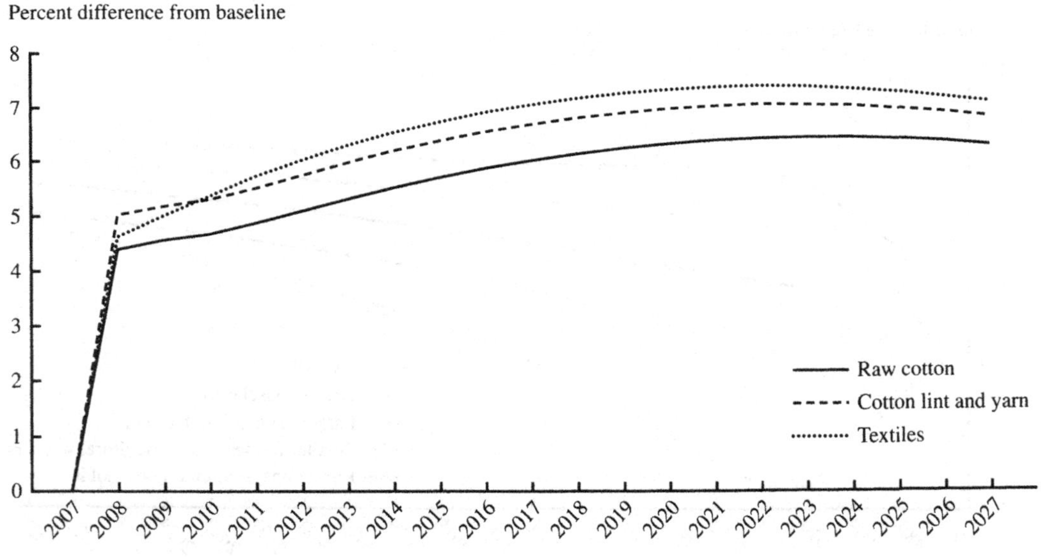

Note: SIM 4c: 5 percent TFP increase in raw cotton, cotton lint and yarn, and textiles.

nificantly higher, with output improving by nearly 5 percent. These effects are sustained in the succeeding years. In the long run the increase in output stabilizes between 6 and 7 percent, which is higher than in the previous two scenarios. This outcome is due to the improved absorptive capacity of the processing sectors for cotton lint and yarn and textiles.

Output prices of the three sectors decline in 2008, with the smallest decrease in textile prices (Figure 9.14). The textile sector benefits from higher cotton lint and yarn production at lower cost. Similarly the cot-

Figure 9.14 Change in output price: SIM 4c

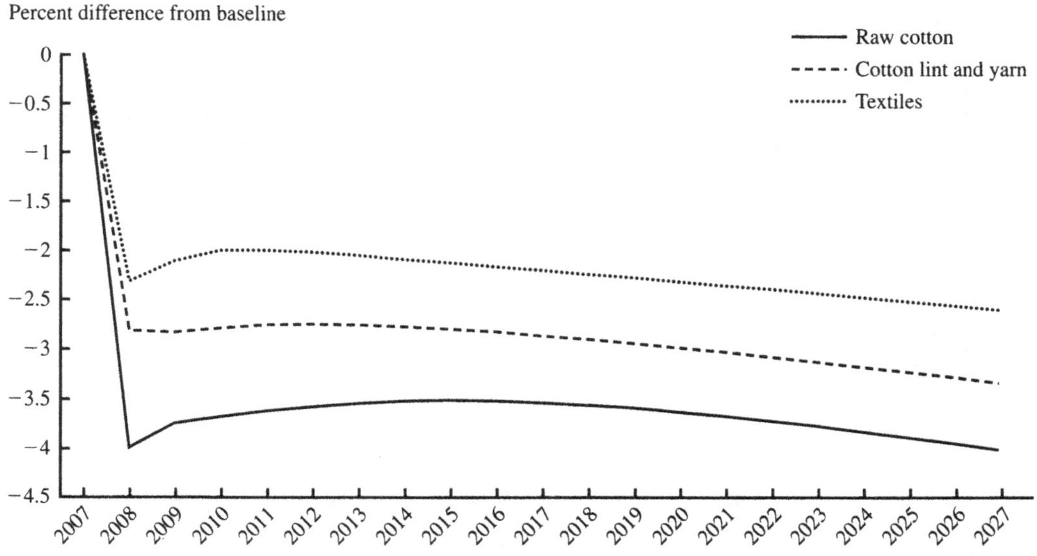

Note: SIM 4c: 5 percent TFP increase in raw cotton, cotton lint and yarn, and textiles.

Figure 9.15 Change in exports: SIM 4c

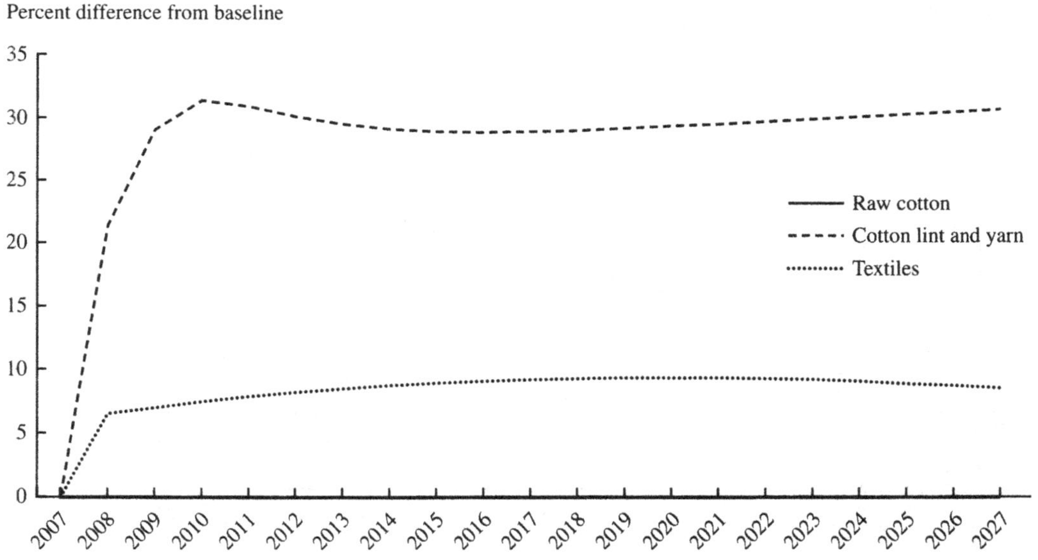

Note: SIM 4c: 5 percent TFP increase in raw cotton, cotton lint and yarn, and textiles.

ton lint and yarn sector benefits from higher raw cotton production at lower cost. Lower production cost also sustains the improvement in exports of both textiles and cotton lint and yarn (Figure 9.15).

The returns to capital in the cotton lint and yarn sector increase from the baseline in the intial years (Figure 9.16). There is a slight drop in returns to capital in raw cotton and textiles in 2008. But the returns to capital in all three cotton-related sectors are positive over an extended period from 2009 to 2019. Therefore higher supply of raw cotton and cotton lint and yarn at lower costs

Figure 9.16 Change in returns to capital: SIM 4c

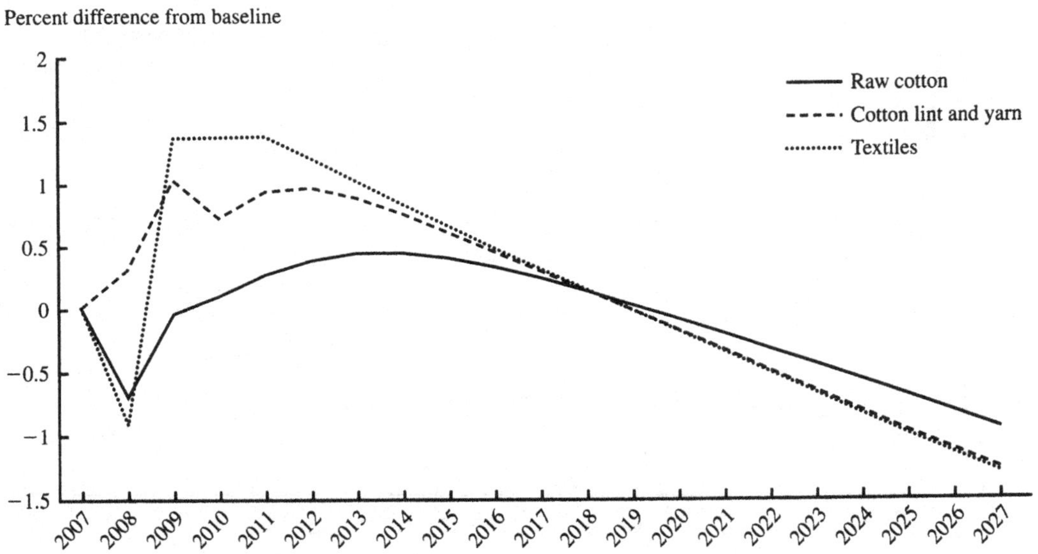

Note: SIM 4c: 5 percent TFP increase in raw cotton, cotton lint and yarn, and textiles.

Figure 9.17 Change in real income: SIM 4c

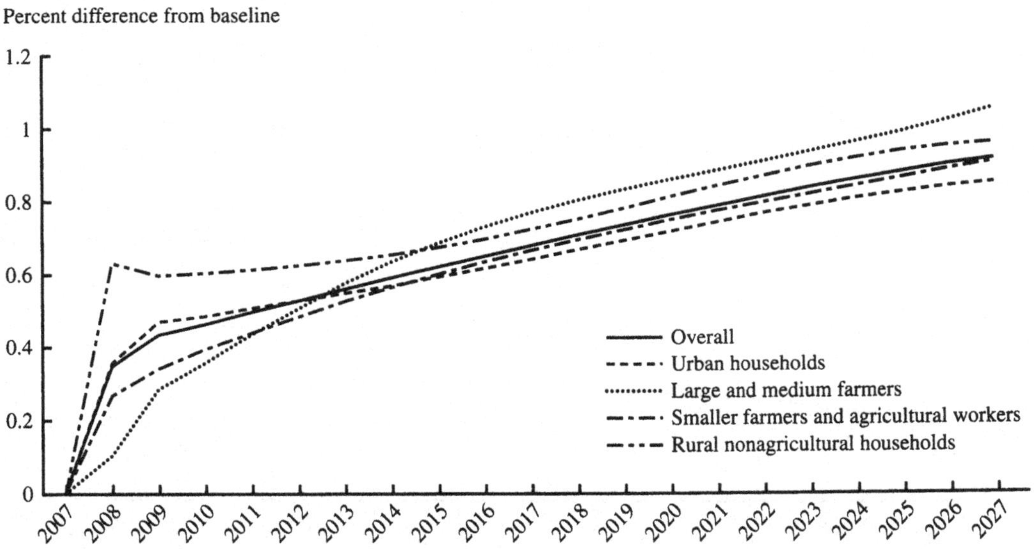

Note: SIM 4c: 5 percent TFP increase in raw cotton, cotton lint and yarn, and textiles.

Figure 9.18 Change in wages and return to land: SIM 4c

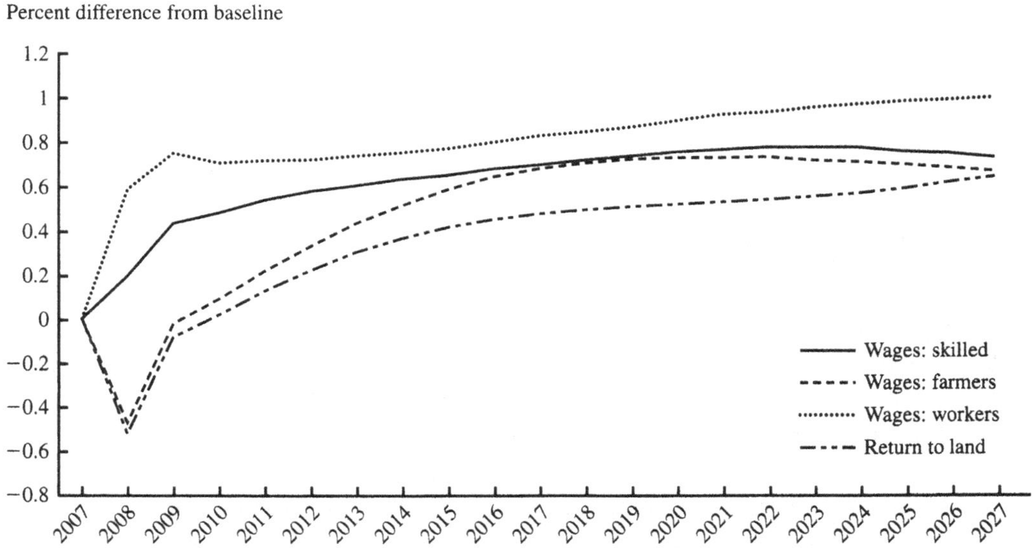

Note: SIM 4c: 5 percent TFP increase in raw cotton, cotton lint and yarn, and textiles.

and inflows of capital into the sectors during these years sustain higher output growth over the baseline.

The effects on household income are presented in Figure 9.17. All household groups benefit from higher income both initially and throughout the simulation period. Large and medium farmers, as well as small farmers and agricultural workers, who suffered from declining income in the first scenario, benefit immediately from higher TFP in all three cotton-related sectors because of higher factor prices relative to the baseline (Figure 9.18).

CHAPTER 10

Summary and Policy Insights

This research report has analyzed some of the key challenges facing the cotton and textile sectors of Pakistan. The first part of the report discussed developments in the international market for cotton, textiles, and apparel. It also described the production and demand structure of the raw cotton, yarn, and textile industries in Pakistan. The second part of the report discussed the simulation results from a CGE model for changes in key variables that affect these sectors. These include changes in the inflows of foreign capital into Pakistan, the world prices of cotton and textiles, the production subsidies to the sectors, and the productivity in the sectors. In this chapter we summarize the important results of the simulations and briefly draw some lessons for policy.

Summary

Table 10.1 summarizes the income and poverty effects across household groups. The greatest increase in household income and reduction in poverty occurs in SIM 1, in which foreign savings increase by 100 percent. Investments improve significantly in this scenario, but the real exchange rate appreciates, resulting in lower exports and higher imports. Production of non-tradables, such as construction, and production in sectors that supply materials to the construction sector, such as cement and bricks, improve. There is significant movement of resources, especially labor, toward these sectors. As a result, factors heavily used in these sectors, such as skilled and unskilled labor and capital, command higher prices. Thus urban households and rural non-farmers benefit. The incidence of urban poverty declines. But the production of tradables, including the products of the cotton lint and textile industries, contracts, and in general the agricultural sector, declines. The wages of farm labor and the average returns to land drop. Despite the drop in the income of rural farmers, the incidence of rural poverty declines because rural non-farmers benefit from the higher wages of unskilled workers and the improvement in the average returns to capital.

The results of SIM 1 may be suggestive of the possible reverse effects of capital outflow. The ongoing political crisis may discourage the continued flow of capital from abroad. The inflow of portfolio investment, which was strong through 2005, may have dried up in fiscal year 2007–08. Although workers' remittances, direct foreign investment, and proceeds from foreign loans remained strong, the inflows were not enough to finance the surge in the foreign trade imbalance as a result of high world food and oil prices. Official reserves were used to close the trade gap. However, this approach will not be sustainable, as the amount of foreign reserves is limited. Thus if the political uncertainty persists and world prices of commodities remain high, a balance-of-payments crisis is possible. This will have unfavorable effects on the real sector of the economy and on poverty.

Table 10.1 Summary of income and poverty results from CGE model simulations

		Urban		Rural					Change in poverty headcount (%)		
							Non-farmers				
	Overall increase in income (%)	All	Poor	All	Farmers	Agricultural workers	All	Poor	All	Urban	Rural
SIM 1	1.31	+	+	+	–	+	+	+	–6.63	–7.41	–6.38
SIM 2a	0.25	–	–	+	+	–	–	–	–0.80	1.90	–1.66
SIM 2b	0.40	+	+	+	–	+	+	+	–0.96	–1.23	–0.87
SIM 2c	0.59	+	–	+	+	–	–	–	–2.01	0.00	–2.65
SIM 3a	–0.05	+	–	–	–	a	a	a	1.05	0.00	1.39
SIM 3b	–0.01	–	–	+	+	–	–	–	0.09	0.47	–0.03
SIM 3c	–0.0013	–	–	+	+	–	–	–	0.11	0.19	0.09
SIM 3d	–0.08	–	+	+	–	+	+	+	–2.45	–1.71	–2.68
SIM 4a[b]	0.40	+	+	+	+[c]	+	+	+			
SIM 4b	0.60	+	+	+	+	+	+	+			
SIM 4c	1.00	+	+	+	+	+	+	+			

Note: SIM 1, increase in foreign savings; SIM 2a, 20 percent increase in world prices of lint and yarn; SIM 2b, 5 percent increase in world prices of textiles; SIM 2c, combination of SIM 2a and 2b; SIM 3a, 5 percent increase in production subsidy in textiles (compensatory consumption tax); SIM 3b, 5 percent increase in production subsidy in cotton lint and yarn (compensatory consumption tax); SIM 3c, 5 percent increase in production subsidy in raw cotton (compensatory consumption tax); SIM 3d, 5 percent increase in production subsidy in textiles (compensatory income tax); SIM 4a, 5 percent TFP increase in raw cotton; SIM 4b, 5 percent TFP increase in raw cotton, and cotton lint and yarn; SIM 4c, 5 percent TFP increase in raw cotton, cotton lint and yarn, and textiles.

[a]Almost zero.

[b]TFP results in SIM 4a to 4c are average long-run change.

[c]In the initial years large and medium farmers will experience negative income change, but the change will be positive in the long run.

The results of SIM 2a, in which the world prices of cotton lint and yarn increase by 20 percent (which is about the magnitude that would have offset the price decrease the Pakistani industries experienced in the late 1990s), indicate an increase in overall household income and a reduction in poverty. However, the effects vary across household groups. Rural farmers benefit from higher wages of farm labor and higher average returns to land. Rural poverty declines. This is due to the demand pull effects on raw cotton production. But the impact on textile production is negative because the increase in the world prices of cotton lint and yarn makes exports relatively profitable compared with domestic sales to the local textile industry. This highlights the dependence of the domestic textile industry on the availability of domestically produced raw materials. The decline in textile production leads to lower prices of factors used in its production, such as skilled labor and capital. As a result urban households and rural non-farmers experience lower income. Urban poverty increases.

We disaggregate the poverty effects under SIM 2a between cotton-producing and non-cotton households in major provinces in Pakistan. There is significant reduction in poverty in cotton households in Punjab, Sindh, and other Pakistan. However, non-cotton households in Sindh and other Pakistan experience an increase in poverty. There are favorable indirect effects of higher world cotton prices in Punjab, the major producer of cotton in Pakistan, with non-cotton households in the province also experiencing lower poverty.

A 5 percent increase in the world prices of textiles in SIM 2b—which again would have offset the decrease in world prices in the late 1990s—leads to an improvement in overall household income and a reduction in poverty. Textile production increases because of higher exports. The increase in production results in higher factor demand and prices of skilled labor and in higher average returns to capital. Thus urban households and rural non-farmers benefit. The increase in textile exports also results in appreciation of the real exchange rate. This makes other sectors, including the cotton lint and yarn sector, less competitive. Exports of cotton lint and yarn decline while imports increase. This decreases the domestic production of cotton lint and yarn, which in turn leads to lower demand for domestically produced raw cotton. Demand for farm labor declines. Wages of farm labor decrease as do the average returns to land. Farmers therefore experience lower income.

Historically the world price of cotton lint has fluctuated more than the world price of yarn and fabric. However, the prices generally move in the same direction. The impact of the joint scenario in SIM 2c—combining a 20 percent increase in the world price of cotton lint and yarn and a 5 percent increase in the world price of textiles—is a relatively higher increase in household income and a greater reduction in poverty.

We analyze the issue of government providing a production subsidy to the cotton-textile sectors in such a way that it does not change the government budget deficit. This is done by fixing the existing government balance and introducing a compensatory tax to finance the subsidy. We introduce both a compensatory consumption tax and a compensatory income tax and compare the results. In all four simulations in Table 10.1 (SIM 3a–3d), there is a reduction in overall welfare, as indicated by the negative change in overall real income. The production subsidy will lower the consumer price of the commodity in question, but it will also increase its producer price index. The compensatory consumption tax will increase the general consumer price index. The increase in poverty under SIM 3a–3c indicates that the increase in the compensatory consumption tax on overall consumer prices will dominate the effect of a subsidy on the cotton-textile sectors when all adjustments in the economy are taken into account. There is, however, a small reduction of 0.03 percent in rural poverty under SIM 3b because of the positive income effects on farmers.

The poverty effects of a compensatory income tax under SIM 3d are much more favorable. This is because, given the structure of the 2001–02 SAM as it reflects flows in the Pakistan economy, it is only the urban non-poor households that shoulder the burden of an additional income tax. The rest of the household groups benefit from the reduction in the consumer price as a result of the subsidy as well as the income transfer from the urban non-poor.

Recent developments in the world market for cotton and textiles present challenges for Pakistan. We address the implications of enhanced international competitiveness of Pakistan in the cotton-textile sectors by assessing the effects of exogenous improvements in TFP. Since improved TFP has long-term implications, we extend our CGE model into a dynamic-recursive form to capture the economywide effects over time. Specifically we generate a baseline scenario without TFP improvement from 2001 to 2027, assuming an increase in the labor supply of 2 percent per year and sectoral capital stock that is updated annually. For each scenario analyzed, we examine the percent difference from the dynamic simulation results with and without TFP improvement to assess the economywide and household income effects. Any increase in TFP is welfare-increasing for all household groups in the long run, as shown in Table 10.1. However, insights can be drawn from the dynamic effects among the cotton-textile sectors and across household groups.

An increase in TFP in raw cotton will improve its output over its baseline values. The increase in production drives down its domestic prices. Because raw cotton is not exported, the effects of productivity improvement are limited by the absorptive capacity of the cotton lint and yarn sector. The cotton lint and yarn sector directly benefits from improved productivity in the raw cotton sector, which induces inflow of capital into the cotton lint and yarn sector. But there is a delayed response in the domestic textiles sector. However, the textiles sector accumulates capital over time, which slowly improves its output. Our results indicate that in about four years the change in output of the textiles sector relative to its baseline values converges to the change in output of raw cotton and cotton lint and yarn sectors over the baseline.

An improvement in TFP in raw cotton increases real income through time. The dynamic interactions across the cotton-related sectors and the rest of the economy cause differential effects on real income across household groups over time. These income effects are due to the change in factor prices. Initially farmers' wages, returns to land, and returns to capital in agriculture decline relative to their baseline values. Thus incomes of large and medium farmers, small farmers, and agricultural workers fall. However, as the other sectors adjust, there is higher income for all household groups because all factor prices improve relative to the baseline values.

An increase in TFP in raw cotton and cotton lint and yarn will improve their output relative to the baseline values. Higher output in both sectors will lead to lower output prices. The level of output of raw cotton rises more than in the previous scenario because of the improvement in its TFP and the increase in the output of cotton lint and yarn, which use raw cotton as input. Thus farm incomes suffer less initial decline and require a shorter adjustment to higher levels. Furthermore there is a surge in exports of cotton lint and yarn because of improved competitiveness. Although the initial effects on the textiles sector are positive, they are minimal. However, as the dynamic effects across the cotton-related sectors and the rest of the economy are seen through 2012, the change in output of these sectors converges to 3.5 percent above the baseline.

An improvement in TFP in all three cotton-related sectors will generate the most positive growth scenario. Each sector will have an immediate and sustained increase in output relative to the baseline. There is a sustained increase in exports of these sectors in the long run because the reduction in their cost of production improves their competitiveness in the export market. Factor prices and household incomes improve most in this scenario.

Overall the results of simulations 1 and 2 demonstrate the different effects arising from two largely external positive shocks—the increase in foreign savings strengthens the currency and creates a boom in the nontrade sectors, whereas an increase in world cotton and textile prices improves Pakistan's terms of trade and generates a boom in the cotton and textile sectors in particular. Because an inflow of foreign savings puts pressure on the exchange rate to appreciate, it depresses the trade sector. Furthermore an exchange rate appreciation will negatively affect household income from foreign remittances. However, it will stimulate investment and a boom in nontraded goods (e.g., activities in construction and private housing will surge). These different effects need to be understood by policymakers trying to assess, for example, the performance of the yarn and textile sectors under more liberalized trade rules but also in light of the capital inflow and increasing foreign remittances. The results of simulations 3 and 4 are relevant to policymakers who must direct limited domestic resources to capacity-building public investments but who also face calls for more direct support from industry lobbies. The analysis of the dynamic effects of TFP improvements highlights the desirability of simultaneous efforts to remove constraints to production across these closely related sectors.

Policy Insights

Owing to the significant size of the cotton-textile sector in Pakistan, as our analysis demonstrates, changes within the industry have significant ripple effects on the rest of the economy and vice versa. As such, policy-makers must have a clear understanding of the economic linkages between the industry and the rest of the economy because major developments are taking place within Pakistan and in the international markets. World cotton prices fell nearly 60 percent between 1994 and 2001, but they recovered by more than 30 percent between 2001 and 2005. The world textile and clothing trade has been liberalized since January 1, 2005. And Pakistan experienced a surge in foreign savings of more than 100 percent after the 9/11 attacks in the United States in 2001. At the same time foreign remittances to households increased from US$1 billion in 2001 to US$4.6 billion in 2005.

While the surge in foreign savings and the improvement in remittances are positive developments for Pakistan, they tend to strengthen the currency, which has negative effects on the competitiveness of the tradable sectors, including the cotton-textile industry. These effects are important to consider because the international markets for textiles and clothing are becoming more price sensitive with liberalization. Under the new international trading arrangements, suppliers that lose competitiveness can expect to suffer losses in market share. Pakistan is competitive in the world market in a number of textile product lines, such as bedwear, towels and cleaning cloths, other textile made-ups, and hosiery. Given the dominance of China in the overall market for textiles and clothing and its potential for further expansion, Pakistan cannot afford to lose competitiveness or its world market share in these product niches.

The improvement in the world prices of cotton and textiles has positive effects on the industry as well as on those households that depend on the industry. Exports increase and drive up domestic production. However, because of the size of cotton and textile exports relative to Pakistan's overall exports, higher exports create pressure on the exchange rate to appreciate. This has negative price effects on tradable sectors outside the cotton-textile-apparel value chain and on household income from abroad. Given Pakistan's limited industrial and manufacturing base, the effort to improve that base through industrial diversification could be hampered if appreciation of the exchange rate is sustained.

The fear of a loss of competitiveness as a result of the abolition of the Multi-Fiber Agreement has led to discussion of increased production subsidies to the cotton-related sectors from the government. But subsidies are welfare-reducing, and financing them with a compensatory consumption tax increases poverty. A better approach to addressing the issue of competitiveness in the cotton-related sectors in Pakistan would be through policies that improve productivity.

There is a need for Pakistan to improve productivity in all stages of the cotton-textile value chain. In raw cotton production, yield must improve. This can be achieved if infestations of cotton viruses and other pests are controlled. The adoption of technological innovations—such as the development of new cotton varieties that are tolerant of insects, including Bt cotton—offers promise. Based on the experiences of India and other major cotton-producing developing countries that adopt Bt cotton technology, cotton yield can improve substantially. Other farm management techniques and best practices suggested by industry analysts could potentially improve yields.

Cotton produced in Pakistan is of low quality because of contamination in various stages of the production and marketing chain. As a result Pakistan produces some of the most contaminated cotton in the world, negatively affecting its price in the international market. To reduce contamination and improve quality would require standardization in the ginning sector. The ginning sector is also in need of upgrades to its antiquated technology, including the primitive saw gins.

The spinning sector produces yarn that is of low count, and this type of yarn commands lower prices in the international market. Thus Pakistan's export earnings for yarn are considerably less than they could be. Furthermore modernization in the production of yarn requires increased use of man-made fibers, since the demand for cotton in the international market has been volatile and there is growing demand for blended (cotton-polyester) fibers. However, the domestic man-made fiber manufacturers in Pakistan are still uncompetitive relative to the world market. The weaving sector is too heavily dependent on cotton fibers. Pakistan is producing less blended fiber than its competitors. Although the production shares of blended fibers and dyed and printed cloth have improved lately, Pakistan still concentrates on the production of gray cloth, which is unprocessed and so commands low prices in the world market.

Investing in productivity improvements—such as the establishment of research and development facilities (which are practically nonexistent in Pakistan), the development of human resources and critical skills, and the adoption of best practices at various stages of the cotton-textile-apparel value chain—will improve total factor productivity and increase income. Such investment would be a far better use of scarce resources than supporting the industry through production subsidies.

APPENDIX A

The Pakistan CGE Model

Model Description

The equations of the CGE model are discussed in this appendix. SIM 1–3 use the one-period, static version of the model. SIM 4 uses the dynamic-recursive version of the model (also called sequential dynamic in the literature). The dynamics in the model are not the result of intertemporal optimization by economic agents. Such agents have myopic behavior. The model is basically a series of static CGE models that are linked between periods by updating procedures for exogenous and endogenous variables.

In the static version capital in all sectors is fixed. Land use in agriculture is also fixed. The supply of skilled labor, unskilled farmers, and workers is also fixed in the static model. In the dynamic version, the supply of all types of labor is allowed to increase by 2 percent per year. Sectoral capital in succeeding periods is not fixed but is updated through a capital accumulation equation that uses sectoral investment and an assumed sectoral depreciation rate. Sectoral investment depends on the sectoral rate of return to capital relative to the user cost of capital. The dynamic model allows land use to vary across agriculture.

The specification of the model is standard, and we discuss some of the key relationships in the model. In equation (1) sectoral output has a fixed coefficient with intermediate input (*CI*) and value added (*VA*). In equation (2) value added in agriculture is a CES function of unskilled labor (*USL*), capital (*K*), and land (*LW*). Value added in the non-agriculture sector in equation (3) is a CES function of skilled labor (*SL*), unskilled labor, and capital. No skilled labor is employed in agriculture, but both skilled and unskilled labor is employed in the non-agriculture sector. Thus skilled labor is mobile only across nonagricultural sectors, while unskilled labor is mobile across all sectors, agricultural and nonagricultural.

In the original 2001–02 SAM, there are 10 labor types (see the footnote to Table 5.5). In the model we lumped together L1–L7 as farm labor. We added L8 and L9 as workers. Farm labor and workers make up unskilled labor in the model. Farm labor is employed only in agriculture, while workers are employed in both agriculture and the non-agriculture sector. L10 is retained as skilled labor. Skilled labor is employed only in the non-agriculture sector.

The demand for skilled labor, derived as the first-order condition, is given in equation (4). Equilibrium in the market for skilled labor in equation (55) equates the total sectoral demand to the supply. This will determine the wage rate for skilled labor. In the dynamic model the supply of skilled labor is updated using equation (60) and an assumed growth of 2 percent per year. The demand for unskilled labor in equation (5) is also derived as the first-order condition.

Unskilled labor in agriculture is a CES composite of farmers and workers in equation (6). In the non-agriculture sector unskilled labor in equation (7) is composed of workers. The demand for farmers in equation (8) is also a first-order condition. The overall demand for farmers is equal to the total supply of farmers in equation (56). This will determine the farm wage. Similarly the total demand for workers is equal to the total supply of workers in equation (57). This will determine the wage rate for workers. The supply of these two labor types is fixed in the static model, but it is updated in the succeeding period in equations (61) and (62) using an assumed growth of 2 percent per year.

The demand for land use in agriculture has two versions: static and dynamic. In the static version we assume fixed land use in each of the agriculture sectors. Thus in equation (9) LW_{ag} is fixed. In each of the agriculture sectors the rate of return to land, rlw_{ag}, is endogenous. Therefore there is one rate of return to land in each of the sectors in agriculture.

In the dynamic model we allow land use to vary across agriculture. There is only one rate of return to land in agriculture in equation (9). This is determined in the land use market equilibrium in equation (58), in which the total demand for land use in agriculture is equal to the supply of land. The total supply of land is fixed in both the static and dynamic models.

In the static model sectoral capital is fixed. The rate of return to capital in each sector is determined endogenously in equation (48) for agriculture and in equation (49) for the non-agriculture sector. These equations also assure zero profit condition in the model. In the dynamic model sectoral capital is updated using the capital accumulation equation (59). In this equation we assume capital stock is measured at the beginning of the period and the flows are measured at the end of the period. We use an investment demand function in equation (18) to determine the flow of new investment into the sector. This equation follows the specification of Bourguignon, Branson, and de Melo (1989) and Jung and Thorbecke (2003). It states that the capital accumulation rate (the ratio of investment demand, *IND,* to capital stock, *K*) is an increasing function of the ratio of the rate of return to capital, *r,* and its user cost, *u.* The user cost is determined in equation (51).

The consumption function in equation (13) is specified as a linear expenditure system. Sectoral output in equation (35) is a CET function of exports (*E*) and domestic demand (*D*). The supply of exports is determined in equation (36). It is a function of the relative price of exports (*Pe*) and local price (*Pl*).[1] The model defines a sectoral composite good, *Q,* using a CES function of imports *D* and *M* in equation (37). The demand for imports is given in equation (38). It is a function of the relative price involving the domestic price (*Pd*) and the import price (*Pm*).[2] The current account balance in equation (39) is the residual between the outflow and the inflow of foreign exchange. The outflow includes import payments, dividend payments to foreigners, and foreign debt service payments, while the inflow includes export receipts, household foreign remittances, and foreign grants to the government.

The import price in domestic currency (*Pm*) is given in equation (40). It is determined by the world price of imports, exchange rate, tariff rate, and indirect tax. The export price is given in equation (41). It is a function of the f.o.b. price of exports and the exchange rate. Exports are perfect substitutes with world outputs.

The price of the composite good for each sector is denoted by *Pq,* which is given by equation (42). The price of output in equation (43) is the weighted price of local price and export price. Note that the difference between the domestic price in equation (44) and the local price is the indirect tax, *itxr.* Equation (45) specifies the value-added price. We define a general price variable

[1] *Pl* does not include indirect tax.

[2] *Pd* includes indirect tax.

called *Pindex,* which is the weighted average sectoral value-added price in equation (47). The price of investment is given in equation (46). Equations (48) and (49) determine the rate of return to capital as noted previously.

Equilibrium in the product market is determined in equation (53). Equation (54) states that total savings—which are composed of household savings, firm savings, government savings, and foreign savings—are invested, which characterizes the model closure.

The numeraire is the nominal exchange rate, *er.* Since we assume that foreign savings in foreign currency, indicated by *CAB* in equation (39), are fixed, all international transactions are cleared by the nominal exchange rate variable. Government savings, *SAVG,* in equation (33) and government total income, *YG,* in equation (31) are both endogenous. However, government consumption in real terms, *GT,* in equation (19) is fixed. Household savings, *SAVH,* in equation (32), as well as household income, *YH,* in equation (25), are both endogenous.

Model Equations

Production

(1) $$X_j = \min\left[\frac{CI_j}{io_j}, \frac{VA_j}{v_j}\right]$$

(2) $$VA_{ag} = \mathbf{K}_{ag}\left(\omega_{usk} USL_{ag}^{-\rho_{vaag}} + \omega_{k} K_{ag}^{-\rho_{vaag}} + \omega_{lw} LW_{ag}^{-\rho_{vaag}}\right)^{\frac{-1}{-\rho_{vaag}}}$$

(3) $$VA_{nag} = \mathbf{K}_{nag}\left(\omega_{sk} SL_{nag}^{-\rho_{vanag}} + \omega_{usk} USL_{nag}^{-\rho_{vanag}} + \omega_{k} K_{nag}^{-\rho_{vanag}}\right)^{\frac{-1}{-\rho_{vanag}}}$$

(4) $$SL_{nag} = VA_{nag}\left(\frac{Pva_{nag}\,\omega_{sk}}{w_{sk}\,\mathbf{K}_{nag}^{\rho_{vanag}}}\right)^{\frac{1}{1+\rho_{vanag}}}$$

(5) $$USL_i = VA_i\left(\frac{Pva_i\,\omega_{usk}}{w_{usk}\,\mathbf{K}_i^{\rho_{va_i}}}\right)^{\frac{1}{1+\rho_{va_i}}}$$

(6) $$USL_{ag} = \mathbf{K}_{uslag}\left(\omega_{wk} WK_{ag}^{-\rho_{uslag}} + \omega_{fr} FR^{-\rho_{uslag}}\right)^{\frac{-1}{\rho_{uslag}}}$$

(7) $$USL_{nag} = WK_{nag}$$

(8) $$FR_{ag} = USL_{ag}\left(\frac{w_{usk}\,\omega_{fr}}{w_{fr}\,\mathbf{K}_{ag}^{\rho_{uslag}}}\right)^{\frac{1}{1+\rho_{uslag}}}$$

(9) $$LW_{ag} = VA_{ag}\left(\frac{Pva_{ag}\,\omega_{lw}}{rlw_{ag}\,\mathbf{K}_{ag}^{\rho_{vaag}}}\right)^{\frac{1}{1-\rho_{vaag}}}$$

(10) $CI_j = io_{ij} X_j$

(11) $mat_{ij} = aij_{ij} CI_j$

Demand

(12) $Ct_h = Dyh_h - Savh_h$

(13) $C_{i,h} = Cmin_{i,h} + \frac{\alpha_{i,h}}{Pq_i}\left(Ct_h - \sum Pq_i Cmin_{i,h}\right)$

(14) $INTD_i = \sum mat_{ij}$

(15) $INV_i = \tau_i \frac{TINV}{Pq_i}$

(16) $TINV = TINVR \cdot Pinv$

(17) $TINVR = \sum IND_i$

(18) $\frac{IND_i}{K_i} = \lambda_i \left(\frac{r_i}{u_i}\right)^2$

(19) $GC_i = \upsilon_i \frac{(GT \cdot Pindex)}{Pq_i}$

Income/Revenue and Savings

(20) $YSL = \sum w_{\mathrm{sk}} SL_{\mathrm{nag}}$

(21) $YLFR = \sum w_{\mathrm{fr}} FR_{\mathrm{ag}}$

(22) $YLWK = \sum w_{\mathrm{wk}} WK_i$

(23) $YK = \sum r K_i$

(24) $YLW = \sum rlw \cdot LW_{\mathrm{ag}}$

(25) $YH_h = YSL \cdot Sh\_SL_h + YLRF \cdot Sh\_FR_h + YLWK \cdot Sh\_WK_h + YK \cdot Sh\_K_h + YLW \cdot Sh\_LW_h + DIV\_H \cdot Sh\_DIV_h \cdot Pindex + TRGOVH_h \cdot Pindex + YFOR \cdot Sh\_YFOR_h \cdot er$

(26) $DYH_h = YH_h(1 - dtxrh_h)$

(27) $YF = YK(Shf\_K)(1 - dtxrf)$

(28) $TMREV = \sum tm_i \cdot M_i \cdot er \cdot Pwm_i$

(29) $DTXREV = \sum dtxrh_h \cdot YH_h + YK(Shf\_K)(dtxrf)$

(30) $ITXREV = \sum itxr_i \cdot D_i \cdot P1_i + \sum itxr_i \cdot M_i \cdot er \cdot Pwm_i (1 + tm_i)$

(31) $YG = TMREV + DTXREV + ITXREV + YLW \cdot Shg\_LW$

(32) $SAVH_h = aps_h DYH_h$

(33) $SAVF = YF - DIV\_H \cdot Pindex - er \cdot DIV\_FOR$

(34) $SAVG = YG - GT \cdot Pindex - \sum TRGOVH_h \cdot Pindex - er \cdot PAYGV\_FOR$

International Trade

(35) $X_i = \mu_i \left(\theta_i E_i^{\rho_{e_i}} + (1 - \theta_i) D_i^{\rho_{e_i}}\right)^{\left(\frac{1}{\rho_{e_i}}\right)}$

(36) $E_i = D_i \left[\frac{Pe_i}{Pl_i} \frac{1 - \theta_i}{\theta_i}\right]^{\sigma_{e_i}}$

(37) $Q_i = \xi_i \left(\delta_i M_i^{-\rho_{m_i}} + (1 - \delta_i) D_i^{-\rho_{m_i}}\right)^{\left(\frac{-1}{\rho_{m_i}}\right)}$

(38) $M_i = D_i \left[\frac{Pd_i}{Pm_i} \frac{1 - \delta_i}{\delta_i}\right]^{\sigma_{m_i}}$

(39) $CAB = \sum Pwm_i \cdot M_i + DIV\_FOR + PAYGV\_FOR - \sum Pwe_i \cdot E_i - \sum YFOR_h -$
$GRANT\_FOR$

Prices

(40) $Pm_i = Pwm_i \cdot er (1 + tm_i)(1 + itxr_i)$

(41) $Pe_i = Pwe_i \cdot er$

(42) $Pq_i Q_i = Pd_i D_i + Pm_i M_i$

(43) $Px_i X_i = Pl_i D_i + Pe_i E_i$

(44) $Pd_i = Pl_i (1 + itxr_i)$

(45) $Pva_i = \frac{(Px_i X_i - \sum mat_{ij} \cdot pq_j)}{VA_i}$

(46) $Pinv = \prod \left[\frac{Pq_i}{\tau_i}\right]^{\tau_i}$

(47) $Pindex = \sum w\_va_i \cdot Pva_i$

(48) $r_{ag} K_{ag} = Pva_{ag} VA_{ag} - w_{usk1} USL_{ag} - rlw_{ag} LN_{ag}$

(49) $r_{nag} Kn_{nag} = Pva_{nag} VA_{nag} - w_{sk} SL_{nag} - w_{uskl} USL_{nag}$

(50) $w_{usk} USL_{ag} = w_{fr} FR_{ag} + w_{wk} WK_{ag}$

(51) $w_{usk} USL_{nag} = w_{wk} WK_{nag}$

(52) $u_i = Pinv(ir + dep_i)$

Equilibrium

(53) $Q_i = INTD_i + \sum_h C_{i,h} + GC_i + INV_i$

(54) $TINV = \sum SAVH_h + SAVF + SAVG + CAB \cdot er$

(55) $SLS = \sum SL_{nag}$

(56) $FRS = \sum FR_{ag}$

(57) $WKS = \sum WK_i$

(58) $LWS + \sum LW_{ag}$

Dynamic Equations

(59) $K_{i,t+1} = K_{i,t}(1 - dep_i) + IND_{i,t}$

(60) $SLS_{t-1} = SLS_t(1 + grw)$

(61) $FRS_{t+1} = FRS_t(1 + grw)$

(62) $WKS_{t+1} = WKS_t(1 + grw)$

Endogenous Variables

CH	commodity consumption of households
CI	intermediate input
CT	total consumption of households
D	domestic demand
DTXREV	direct tax revenue
DYH	disposable income
E	exports
er	nominal exchange rate
FR	unskilled farmers
GC	sectoral real government consumption
GT	nominal total government consumption
IND	demand for capital, by destination
INTD	intermediate demand
INV	investment demand, by origin
ITXREV	indirect tax revenue
K	capital
LW	land
M	imports
mat	interindustry matrix
Pd	domestic price
Pe	export price
Pinv	price of investment
Pl	local prices
Pm	import price

Pq	composite price of commodity
Pva	value-added price
Pwe	f.o.b. prices of exports
Px	output price
Q	composite demand, domestic and imports
r	return to capital
rlw_{ag}	return to land
SAVF	firm savings
SAVG	government savings
SAVH	household savings
SL	skilled labor
TINV	nominal total investment
TINVR	real total investment
TMREV	tariff revenue
u	user cost of capital
USL	unskilled labor
VA	value added
w_{fr}	wage for farm labor
WK	unskilled workers
w_{sk}	wage for skilled labor
w_{usk}	average wage for unskilled labor
w_{wk}	wage for workers
X	output
YF	firm income
YG	government income
YH	household income
YK	capital income
YLFR	income from farmers
YLW	land income
YLWK	income from unskilled workers
YSL	income from skilled labor

Exogenous Variables

CAB	current account balance or foreign savings
dep	depreciation rate
DIV_FOR	dividends paid to foreigners
DIV_H	total dividend income of households
dtxrf	income tax rate of firms
dtxrh	direct income tax rate of households
E0	export at the base
FRS	supply of farm labor
GRANT_FOR	foreign grants to government
ir	real interest rate
itxr	indirect tax rates
PAYGV_FOR	debt service payment of government
Pindex	weighted value-added price
Pwe0	world price of exports
Pwm	world price of imports
SLS	supply of skilled labor
tm	tariff rate
TRGOVH	government transfers to household
WKS	supply of workers
YFOR	foreign income of households

All other notations represent elasticities and calibrated share and scale parameters, which are fixed. The following sets are used: (*i*, *j*) = production sectors; ag = agricultural sectors; nag = nonagricultural sectors; *h* = households.

APPENDIX B

Substitution Parameters in Cotton-Related Sectors

We introduce a 20 percent increase in world prices of cotton lint under various combinations of factor substitution and export and import parameters in raw cotton, cotton lint and yarn, and textile sectors, and we examine and compare the quantity and price responses with the actual price movements. We assume that an increase in world prices of cotton lint will affect both world export and import prices of this commodity. For the factor substitution elasticity we alter $\sigma_{va} = 1 + 1/\rho_{va}$ in the CES production function in equations (2) and (3) in Appendix A. For the import function we alter $\sigma_m = 1 + 1/\rho_m$ in equation (36), while for the export function we change $\sigma_e = 1 + 1/\rho_e$ in equation (34). Here we examine the results of two cases.

Case 1

(1a) σ_{va} = 0.75 for raw cotton; = 1.5 for cotton lint and yarn; = 1.5 for textiles
(1b) σ_e = 2 for cotton lint and yarn; = 2 for textiles
(1c) σ_m = 1.5 for cotton lint and yarn; = 1.5 for textiles

Case 2

(2a) σ_{va} =2.25 for raw cotton; = 1.25 for cotton lint and yarn; = 1.25 for textiles
(2b) σ_e = 25 for cotton lint and yarn; = 25 for textiles
(2c) σ_m = 25 for cotton lint and yarn; = 25 for textiles
(2d) for the rest of the sectors, retain all elasticity parameters in Table 5.1

The results are given in Table B.1. In case 1 the export price of cotton lint and yarn increases by 17.3 percent, while its output price improves by 8.8 percent. The price ratio is 0.5. This is very far from the ratios we find in Table 3.5, in which the market price does not deviate much from the export parity price. Furthermore the output price of raw cotton improves by 15.3 percent, significantly higher than the 8.8 percent increase in the output price of cotton lint and yarn. The ratio is 1.74. This ratio is high compared with the historical ratio presented in Figure B.1. In the past five years, the percent change in seed prices relative to the percent change in cotton yarn prices is 0.66.

In case 2 the export price of cotton lint and yarn improves by 17.75 percent. Its output price increases by 16.43 percent. The ratio is 0.926, which is higher than in case 1 and nearer to 1. Furthermore the output price of raw cotton improves by 13.02 percent. Thus the output price ratio of raw cotton over cotton lint and yarn is 0.79, which is relatively nearer to the historical ratio. Thus we consider the elasticities in case 2.

Table B.1 Sectoral effects under various elasticity parameters (percent change from base)

	Case 1	Case 2
Real exchange rate	–1.61	–0.93
Domestic price	0.05	0.30
Raw cotton		
Output	4.80	7.31
Output price	11.13	8.03
Cotton lint and yarn		
Output	5.42	8.26
Domestic demand	0.36	–0.54
Export	18.47	31.76
Output price	6.75	10.09
Export price	13.17	10.96
Textiles		
Output	–2.90	–5.04
Output price	–0.30	–0.72

Figure B.1 Price movements of seed cotton and yarn (percent)

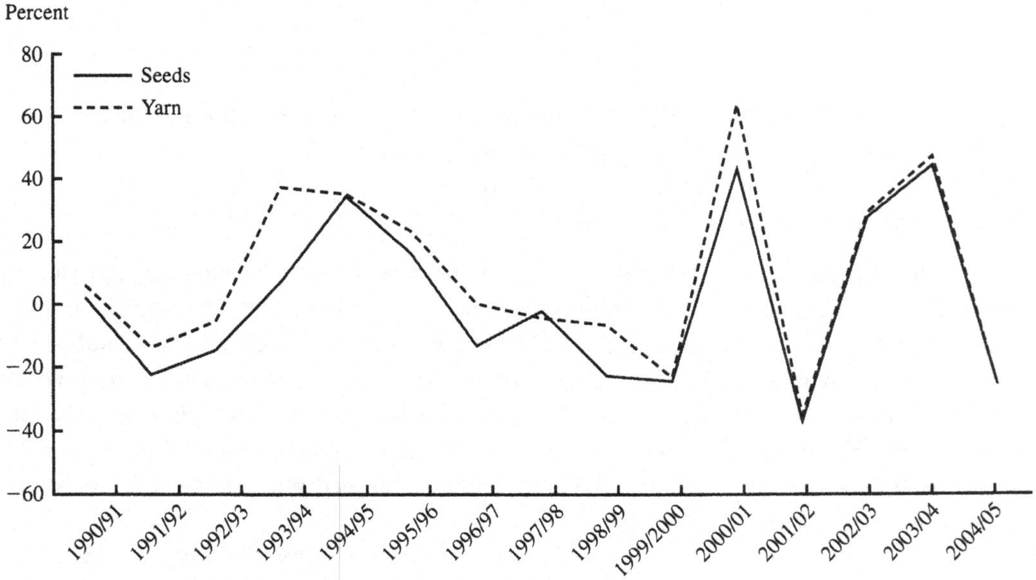

References

Altaf, Z. 2008. Challenges in the Pakistan cotton, yarn, textile and apparel sectors. In *Cotton-textile-apparel sectors of Pakistan: Situation and challenges faced,* ed. C. B. Cororaton, A. Salam, Z. Altaf, and D. Orden. IFPRI Discussion Paper. Washington, D.C.: International Food Policy Research Institute.

Annabi, N., J. Cockburn, and B. Decaluwé. 2006. Functional forms and parameterization of CGE models. Modeling and Policy Impact Analysis Working Paper Series 2006-04. <http://www.pepnet.org/>.

Annabi, N., B. Khonder, S. Raihan, J. Cockburn, and B. Decaluwé. 2006. Implications of WTO agreements and unilateral trade policy reforms for poverty in Bangladesh: Short- versus long-run impacts. In *Poverty and the WTO: Impacts of the Doha development agenda,* ed. T. Hertel and L. A. Winters. Houndmills, Basingstoke, U.K.: Palgrave Macmillan and World Bank.

Asian Development Bank. 2007. Key indicators 2007: Inequality in Asia. <http://www.adb.org/Documents/Books/Key_Indicators/2007/default.asp>.

Baffes, J. 2004. Cotton: Market setting, trade policies, and issues. In *Global agricultural trade and developing countries,* ed. M. Aksoy and J. Beghin. Washington, D.C.: World Bank.

Bedi, J., and C. B. Cororaton, eds. 2008. *Cotton-textile-apparel sectors of India: Situation and challenges faced.* IFPRI Discussion Paper. Washington, D.C.: International Food Policy Research Institute.

Bourguignon, F., W. H. Branson, and J. de Melo. 1989. *Macroeconomic adjustment and income distribution: A macro-micro simulation model.* Organisation for Economic Cooperation and Development (OECD) Technical Paper 1. Paris: OECD.

CIE (Centre for International Economics). 2001. Trade distortions and cotton markets: Implications for Australia cotton producers. Report prepared for the Cotton Research and Development Corporation, Canberra, Australia.

Cockburn, J. 2001. *Trade liberalisation and poverty in Nepal: A computable general equilibrium micro simulation analysis.* Centre de Recherche en Économie et Finance Appliquées, Université Laval, Discussion Paper 01-18. Québec, Canada.

Cockburn, J., I. Fofana, B. Decaluwé, R. Mabugu, and M. Chitiga. 2006. A gender-focused macro-micro analysis of the poverty impacts of trade liberalization in South Africa. *Research on Economic Inequality* 15: 269–305.

Cororaton, C. B., and J. Cockburn. 2007. Trade reform and poverty—Lessons from the Philippines: A CGE microsimulation analysis. *Journal of Policy Modeling* 29 (1): 141–163.

Cororaton, C. B., J. Cockburn, and E. Corong. 2006. Doha scenarios, trade reforms, and poverty in the Philippines: A CGE analysis. In *Poverty and the WTO: Impacts of the Doha development agenda,* ed. T. Hertel and L. A. Winters. Houndmills, Basingstoke, U.K.: Palgrave Macmillan and World Bank.

Cororaton, C. B., A. Salam, Z. Altaf, and D. Orden, eds. 2008. *Cotton-textile-apparel sectors of Pakistan: Situation and challenges faced.* IFPRI Discussion Paper. Washington, D.C.: International Food Policy Research Institute.

Dawn, the Internet Edition. 2007. BT cotton variety to be released next season. <http://www.dawn.com/2007/01/05/ebr8.htm>.

Decaluwé, B., J. C. Dumont, and V. Robichaud. 2000. MIMAP training session on CGE modeling, Volume 2: Basic CGE models. <http://www.pepnet.org/>.

Decaluwé, B., J. C. Dumont, and L. Savard. 1999. *Measuring poverty and inequality in a computable general equilibrium model.* Centre de Recherche en Économie et Finance Appliquées (CREFA), Université Laval, Working Paper 99-20. Québec, Canada: CREFA.

De Janvry, A., E. Sadoulet, and A. Fargeix. 1991. Politically feasible and equitable adjustment: Some alternatives for Ecuador. *World Development* 19 (11): 1577–1594.

Dorosh, P., M. K. Niazi, and H. Nazli. 2004. *A social accounting matrix for Pakistan, 2001–02: Methodology and results.* Background research paper for Pakistan Rural Factor Markets Study. South Asia Rural Development Unit. Washington, D.C.: World Bank.

Economic Research Service, U.S. Department of Agriculture (USDA). 2007. Cotton and wool yearbook. <http://www.ers.usda.gov/data/fibertextiletrade/>.

Emini, C., J. Cockburn, and B. Decaluwé. 2006. The poverty impacts of the Doha Round in Cameroon: The role of tax policy. In *Poverty and the WTO: Impacts of the Doha development agenda,* ed. T. Hertel and L. A. Winters. Houndmills, Basingstoke, U.K.: Palgrave Macmillan and World Bank.

FAO (Food and Agriculture Organization). 2004. *Cotton—Impact of support policies on developing countries: A guide to contemporary analysis.* Trade Policy Brief 1. Rome.

———. 2006. Cotton commodity notes. <www.fao.org/es/ESC/en/15/304/highlight_307.html>.

Federal Bureau of Statistics. 2003. Household Integrated Economic Survey: Round 4, 2001–02. Islamabad: Government of Pakistan.

Foster, J., J. Greer, and E. Thorbecke. 1984. A class of decomposable poverty measures. *Econometrica* 52 (3): 761–766.

Ganuza, E., R. Barros, and R. Vos. 2002. Labor market adjustment, poverty and inequality during liberalization. In *Economic liberalization, distribution and poverty: Latin America in the 1990s,* ed. R. Vos, L. Taylor, and R. Paes de Barros. Cheltenham, U.K., and Northampton, Mass., U.S.A.: Edward Elgar.

Gillson, I., C. Poulton, K. Balcombe, and S. Page. 2004. *Understanding the impact of cotton subsidies on developing countries.* London: Overseas Development Institute.

Goreaux, L. 2003. Prejudice caused by industrialized countries subsidies to cotton sector in Western and Central Africa. Background document to the submission made by Benin, Burkina Faso, Chad, and Mali to the World Trade Organization (WTO). World Trade Organization, Geneva.

Government of Pakistan. 2000. Agriculture Census 2000. Lahore: Agriculture Census Organization.

———. 2003. Pakistan Economic Survey 2002–2003. Islamabad: Ministry of Finance.

———. 2004. Pakistan Economic Survey 2003–2004. Islamabad: Ministry of Finance.

———. 2006a. Pakistan Economic Survey 2004–2005. Islamabad: Ministry of Finance.

———. 2006b. Agricultural statistics of Pakistan, 2004–2005. Islamabad: Ministry of Food, Agriculture, and Livestock.

———. 2008. Pakistan Economic Survey 2007–2008. Islamabad: Ministry of Finance.

ICAC (International Cotton Advisory Committee). 2002. *Cotton: World statistics.* Washington, D.C.

———. 2003. *Production and trade policies affecting the cotton industry.* Washington, D.C.

———. 2007. *Cotton: World statistics.* Washington, D.C.

IMF (International Monetary Fund). 2008. Primary commodity prices. Washington, D.C. <http://www.imf.org/external/np/res/commod/table2.pdf>.

Jung, H. S., and Thorbecke E. 2003. The impact of public education expenditure on human capital, growth, and poverty in Tanzania and Zambia: A general equilibrium approach. *Journal of Policy Modeling* 25: 701–725.

Keeney, R., and T. Hertel. 2004. *GTAP-AGR: A framework for assessing the implications of multilateral changes in agricultural policies.* GTAP Technical Paper 24. West Lafayette, Ind., U.S.A.: Purdue University. <https://www.gtap.agecon.purdue.edu/resources/tech_papers.asp>.

Lofgren, H., R. Harris, S. Robinson, M. Thomas, and M. El-Said. 2002. *A standard computable general equilibrium (CGE) model in GAMS.* Washington, D.C.: International Food Policy Research Institute.

Martin, W. 2004. Textile and clothing policy note: Implications for Pakistan of abolishing textile and clothing export quotas. Manuscript. Washington, D.C.: World Bank.

Nordias, H. 2004. *The global textile and clothing industry post the agreements of textiles and clothing.* Discussion Paper 5. Geneva: World Trade Organization.

Orden, D., A. Salam, R. Dewina, H. Nazli, and N. Minot. 2008. The impact of global cotton and wheat markets on rural poverty in Pakistan. In *Cotton-textile-apparel sectors of Pakistan: Situations and challenges,* ed. C. B. Cororaton, A. Salam, Z. Altaf, and David Orden. IFPRI Discussion Paper. Washington, D.C.: International Food Policy Research Institute.

Poonyth, D., A. Sarris, R. Sharma, and S. Shui. 2004. *The impact of domestic and trade policies on the world cotton market.* FAO Commodity and Trade Policy Research Working Paper 8. Rome: FAO.

Reeves, G., D. Vincent, D. Quirke, and S. Wyatt. 2001. Trade distortion and cotton market: Implications for Australian cotton producers. Report prepared for the Cotton Research and Development Corporation, Canberra, Australia, by the Center for International Economics, College Park, Md., U.S.A.

Robinson, S., M. El-Said, N. San, S. Hermanto, D. Swastika, and S. Bahri. 1997. *Rice price policies in Indonesia: A computable general equilibrium analysis.* TMD Discussion Paper 19. Washington, D.C.: International Food Policy Research Institute.

Salam, A. 2008. Production, prices, and emerging challenges in the Pakistan cotton sector. In *Cotton-textile-apparel sectors of Pakistan: Situations and challenges,* ed. C. B. Cororaton, A. Salam, Z. Altaf, and D. Orden. IFPRI Discussion Paper. Washington, D.C.: International Food Policy Research Institute.

State Bank of Pakistan. 2008. Economic data. Karachi. <http://www.sbp.org.pk/ecodata/index2.asp>.

Sumner, D. 2003. A quantitative simulation-analysis of the impacts of U.S. cotton subsidies on cotton prices and quantities. <www.mre.gov.br/portugues/ministerio/sitios_secretaria/cgc/analisequantitativa.pdf>.

Tokarick, S. 2003. *Measuring the impact of distortions in agricultural trade in partial and general equilibrium.* International Monetary Fund (IMF) Working Paper WP/03/110. Washington, D.C.: IMF.

Townsend, T., and A. Gutichounts. 1994. A survey of income and price support programs. In *Proceedings, beltwide cotton production research conferences.* Memphis, Tenn., U.S.A.: National Cotton Council of America.

United Nations Statistics Division. 2006. Commodity trade statistics database. <http://www.comtrade.un.org/>.

World Bank. 2007. *Pakistan: Promoting rural growth and poverty reduction.* Sustainable Development Unit and South Asia Region. Washington, D.C.

World Trade Organization. 2007. International trade statistics. <http://www.wto.org/english/res_e/statis_e/its2007_e/its07_toc_e.htm>.

Made in the USA
Monee, IL
05 November 2026

67379917R00070